To MY
BEST FRIEND.
Merry Christmas
2015
Love you always
Paula xx
:)

THE GREAT AUSTRALIAN COOKBOOK

Reg Mombassa

EDITORS Helen Greenwood & Melissa Leong

PHOTOGRAPHY Lottie Hedley   **CREATIVE DIRECTION** Tim Harper   **COVER ART** Reg Mombassa

thom & PQ Blackwell

CONTENTS

We think this book is more than just a cookbook. For us, this book is an affectionate snapshot of Australia and the food we love to eat. To take this picture of Australia's ways of cooking and eating, we began, over many cups of tea and biscuits, by writing out the names of chefs, cooks, bakers and food heroes we admire. We whittled down a list as long as the Stuart Highway to just 100 — not an easy task — and asked them: "What do you cook for the people you love?" Then we crossed our fingers.

As it turns out, there was no need to cross anything. Without hesitation, these celebrated restaurant chefs and beloved cooks, dedicated farmers and fishers, wondrous pastry cooks, and hard-working bakers and food-makers told us. They bowled us over with their willingness to share their thoughts, their time and their recipes.

Margaret Fulton with her daughter, Suzanne Gibbs, honoured us by whipping up a classic sponge with strawberries and cream. Charmaine Solomon welcomed us with a festive Sri Lankan meal, her daughters, Deborah and Nina, by her side. Stephanie Alexander lifted the lid on a casserole and happily inhaled her 'simplest beef stew'. Neil Perry bundled up spicy prawns in soft tortillas while his youngest daughters hung over his restaurant's kitchen pass. Peter 'G'day' Russell-Clarke put down his paintbrush long enough to pick up the bones of a smoked trout and boil up a clear, rich soup.

To capture these moments, our travelling team — led by creative director Tim Harper along with co-editor Melissa Leong, photographer Lottie Hedley and videographer Hayley Thom — followed the compass needle from Sydney and Melbourne into the heart of the country. They watched Ross O'Meara twice-cook wallaby shanks on Bruny Island in Tasmania; Dan Hunter roast a chook in Birregurra in Victoria; Clayton Donovan squeeze finger-lime pearls onto open oysters in Nambucca Heads in New South Wales; and Maggie Beer celebrate quinces in a tart in South Australia's Barossa Valley.

In Far North Queensland's Daintree, the foursome sniffed the vanilla- and cinnamon-scented air on Josette and George Gonthier's plantation, where the couple burned their cinnamon wood in an old washing machine drum to make fragrant barbecued chicken. In the west, Jim 'The Sardine Man' Mendolia took them out on his sardine boat at sunrise off the Fremantle coast and dolphins (truly) came out to play.

A streaky, pastel dawn greeted our travellers in the Northern Territory's Rainbow Valley as Max Emery stooped over a campfire in the sandy-red dirt and banged out a bush tomato-studded damper. A fiery-orange sunset unrolled for hours as they sank a cold beer or three at Ross and Jane Fargher's Prairie Hotel in outback South Australia. Six months, thousands of kilometres, one epic journey. Along the way, we were treated to massive helpings of hospitality and serves of kindness for which we are grateful; the happy result is in your hands.

We're delighted that OzHarvest will receive royalties from sales of the book to support its work nourishing those in need, and we're in awe of the legendary Reg Mombassa, whose iconic art adorns it. Last but very much not least, to all the amazing contributors whose generosity overflows in these pages, we thank you. This book is for all Australians who want to cook with love and for love – which makes for the best kind of food, wouldn't you say?

Happy reading and happy cooking,

Helen Greenwood and Melissa Leong

MAX EMERY
DESERT GARDEN PRODUCE

BUSH TOMATO DAMPER

I love living in the desert for its isolation and freedom. As a scientist, I can do all my studies away from everything. There's presently a population of five people out here. If it increases, I may have to move further inland.

Max - Rainbow Valley

RAINBOW VALLEY, NT

BUSH TOMATO DAMPER

SERVINGS: 8–10 | PREP TIME: 10 MINS PLUS HEATING COALS
COOK TIME: 25 MINS | SKILL LEVEL: 1 (EASY)

INGREDIENTS

3 cups self-raising flour

¼ tsp salt

1 tsp sugar

80 g cold butter, cubed

2 tbsp ground dried
bush tomato

180 ml milk

a few whole bush
tomatoes (if available),
for garnishing

METHOD

Prepare a fire to make hot coals for your damper. Grease and flour a camp oven.

Place flour, salt and sugar in a bowl, then rub butter into flour mixture until it resembles breadcrumbs. Add in ground bush tomato and mix through.

Make a well in the centre of the mixture and add milk, slowly turning the mixture until it is a soft dough. Knead gently on a floured surface.

Shape into a round loaf to fit the circumference of your camp oven. If garnishing, press the whole bush tomatoes into the top of the dough. Place dough into camp oven and cover with lid.

Dig a hole near your fire, place hot coals at the base and cover with dirt. Place camp oven in the hole, put some sand on top of camp oven lid, and top with some more hot coals.

Leave to bake for 25 minutes, or until a skewer come out clean and damper has a hollow sound when tapped.

Serve warm with butter and treacle or your favourite jam.

MARGARET FULTON OAM
& SUZANNE GIBBS

HONEY SPICE ROLL
CLASSIC SPONGE CAKE

All of us Fulton women have fond memories of being happy in the kitchen and I think children should be introduced to the kitchen at a very early age. Even the smallest member of the family can have a job, even if its just shelling peas. Children who grow up in the kitchen and slowly learn to cook, enjoy growing up learning the simple joy of appreciation for their efforts. It makes you feel good as a young person ... and a not-so-young person too!

Margaret Fulton

BALMAIN,
NSW

HONEY SPICE ROLL

SERVINGS: 6–8 | PREP TIME: 30 MINS | COOK TIME: 20 MINS | SKILL LEVEL: 1 (EASY)

INGREDIENTS

4 eggs, separated
½ cup (110 g) caster
  sugar, plus 1 tbsp
  extra to dust
½ cup (75 g) cornflour
3 tbsp plain flour
3 tsp baking powder
1 tsp mixed spice
½ tsp ground cinnamon
¼ cup liquid honey,
  at room temperature
180 ml thickened cream

METHOD

Pre-heat the oven to 180°C (or 160°C fan-forced). Lightly grease and line the base and sides of a 23 cm x 32 cm Swiss roll tin.

Using an electric mixer, beat egg whites until firm but not dry. Add the ½ cup of sugar, 1 tbsp at a time, beating constantly until mixture is thick and glossy. Beat in egg yolks until just combined.

Sift together cornflour, flour, baking powder, mixed spice and cinnamon. Lightly fold into egg mixture with 1 tbsp of honey, until evenly distributed. Fill prepared tin, shaking gently to spread mixture evenly.

Bake for 20 minutes, until sponge springs back when lightly touched. Turn out onto a tea towel lightly dusted with extra caster sugar. Peel off paper and trim edges. Roll sponge up immediately in a tea towel, starting from a short edge. Set aside to cool.

Whip cream with remaining honey. Unroll cake and spread cream over. Roll up again and cover with plastic wrap. Chill in the fridge for 30 minutes, then cut into slices to serve.

CLASSIC SPONGE CAKE

SERVINGS: 6–8 | PREP TIME: 20 MINS | COOK TIME: 30 MINS | SKILL LEVEL: 1 (EASY)

INGREDIENTS

95 g self-raising flour
25 g cornflour
4 eggs, separated
100 g caster sugar,
  plus 2 tbsp extra
1 tsp vanilla extract
¼ tsp cream of tartar
300 ml cream, whipped
1 punnet strawberries,
  hulled and sliced, to fill
icing sugar, to dust

METHOD

Pre-heat the oven to 200°C. Grease and line the base of a 22 cm cake tin. Sift the flour and cornflour together, and set aside.

Using an electric mixer, whisk together egg yolks, the 100 g caster sugar and vanilla for 2–3 minutes, until thick and mousse-like. Set aside.

Whisk egg whites until starting to froth, then add cream of tartar and continue to whisk until stiff but not dry. Whisk in the 2 tablespoons of sugar gradually.

Fold a large scoop of whisked egg white into the beaten yolks, to slacken the mixture, then fold in the sifted flour and finally the remaining egg whites, until just combined.

Turn the mixture into the prepared tin, gently smoothing the top. Place in the oven, reducing the temperature to 170°C, and bake for 30 minutes. Check if the cake is cooked before taking it out of the oven by very gently pressing with an index finger to check if the centre of the cake is firm. If so, remove from the oven and check the centre with a very fine cake skewer – it should come out clean. Leave to cool in the tin for 5 minutes before removing to cool completely on a wire rack, to make sure the top is nicely set.

Once cooled, split the cake by cutting with a sharp serrated knife into two even rounds. Top the base with whipped cream and strawberries, then place the cake top on.

When ready to serve, dust with icing sugar.

TIP

Instead of splitting one sponge, this classic cake can be made by baking two sponges and sandwiching them with the cream and strawberries.

SHARON & CAROL SALLOUM
ALMOND BAR

TABOULI
BABA GHANOUJ
HUMMUS
LAHEM MESHWI

FAMILY GATHERINGS ARE RAUCOUS AFFAIRS
THAT LAST LONG INTO THE NIGHT AND
HAPPEN NOT NEARLY AS OFTEN AS ANYONE
WOULD LIKE. OUR DAD'S GREATEST BBQ
TIP IS THAT YOU SHOULD LEARN THE
ART OF MAKING PEOPLE FEEL WELCOME
WHILST MAKING SURE YOU DON'T BURN
THE MEAT! — SHARON + CAROL

GRANVILLE,
NSW

TABOULI
MIDDLE EASTERN PARSLEY & BURGHUL WHEAT SALAD

SERVINGS: 4–6 | PREP TIME: 40 MINS | SKILL LEVEL: 1 (EASY)

INGREDIENTS

4 bunches flat-leaf parsley
⅓ cup (55 g)
  fine white burghul
handful of mint leaves,
  finely chopped
4 spring onions, root end
  trimmed, finely sliced
3 firm medium tomatoes,
  finely diced

Dressing
¼ cup (60 ml) lemon juice
¼ cup (60 ml) extra virgin
  olive oil
2 tsp salt flakes
½ tsp freshly ground
  black pepper
½ tsp sweet paprika

METHOD

Rinse the parsley under cold water to remove any dirt, then leave it to dry for about 10 minutes. It's best to cut two bunches at a time. Remove the stalks from just under the bottom leaves. Hold the two bunches tightly together against the chopping board and, with a very sharp knife, carefully cut the parsley as finely as you can. Rinse the chopped parsley in cold water to remove any remaining dirt and fine particles, then squeeze with your hands and spread the washed parsley out on a clean tea towel. Leave to dry at room temperature for 20–30 minutes.

Meanwhile, place the burghul in a small bowl with 100 ml water. Set aside for about 15 minutes to allow the burghul to soak up the water and soften slightly.

To make the dressing, place all the ingredients in a small bowl and mix together well.

Place the parsley, mint, spring onion, tomato and soaked burghul in a medium bowl. Pour the dressing over the top and toss to combine well. Serve immediately.

BABA GHANOUJ
SMOKED EGGPLANT DIP

MAKES: JUST OVER 2 CUPS (ABOUT 450 G) | PREP TIME: 30 MINS | SKILL LEVEL: 1 (EASY)

INGREDIENTS

2 eggplants
½ cup (140 g) tahini
¼ cup (60 ml) lemon juice
1 clove garlic, crushed
2 tsp salt flakes
sumac, for sprinkling
finely diced tomato
  and olive oil, to garnish

METHOD

Prick each eggplant with a fork in three places. Using tongs, turn the eggplants over an open gas stovetop flame until they are charred all over and the skin is starting to crack. The whole point is to burn the skin, so do not worry when this happens. Place the charred eggplants in a bowl of cold water to cool for about 10 minutes, then hold them under a slow stream of cold running water, and remove the stalks and peel off the blackened skin. Open the eggplants and remove as many seeds as possible from the centre. You may not be able to take out every last seed; just do your best as this will help rid the eggplant of any bitterness. Once cleaned, place the eggplant in a colander to drain.

Place the eggplant, tahini, lemon juice, garlic and salt in a food processor and blend for 3–4 minutes or until well combined. The baba ghanouj should not be completely smooth – slightly lumpy is good, but you don't want any big chunks of eggplant in the mix. Scrape down the sides of the bowl and pulse a couple of times.

Spoon the baba ghanouj into a shallow bowl and garnish with a sprinkling of sumac, some finely diced tomato and a drizzle of olive oil. Serve with Middle Eastern or your choice of bread. Store in an airtight container in the fridge for up to four days.

HUMMUS
CHICKPEA DIP

MAKES: JUST UNDER 2 CUPS (ABOUT 500 G) | PREP TIME: 10 MINS PLUS SOAKING
COOK TIME: 50 MINS PLUS COOLING | SKILL LEVEL: 1 (EASY)

INGREDIENTS

½ tsp bicarbonate of soda
1 cup (200 g)
   dried chickpeas
½ cup (140 g) hulled tahini
juice of 2 lemons
1 small clove garlic, crushed
½ tsp salt flakes,
   or to taste
extra virgin olive oil
   and sweet paprika,
   to garnish (optional)

METHOD

Dissolve the bicarbonate of soda in a large bowl of water, add the chickpeas and soak overnight. Rinse and drain.

Place the chickpeas in a medium-sized saucepan and cover generously with water (the water should be double the amount of chickpeas). Cook over a high heat. Once the water starts to boil, reduce the heat to low and remove any scum that may have appeared on the surface. Cook for about 40 minutes, or until the chickpeas are tender and can be crushed between two fingers. Drain and allow to cool.

Place the cooled chickpeas in a food processor and blend until as smooth as possible. You may need to add a couple of splashes of water to bring the chickpeas together if they start sticking to the side of the processor. Add the tahini, lemon juice, garlic and salt, and blend until well combined.

At this point the dip will become quite thick and difficult to blend. Gradually add enough water to thin it out to a smooth paste – start with 2 tablespoons and take it from there. Don't add too much, or it will turn into a sauce. Taste and add more salt if preferred.

Transfer the hummus to a shallow bowl and finish with a drizzle of olive oil and a sprinkling of sweet paprika. Serve with Middle Eastern or your choice of bread.

Store in an airtight container in the fridge for up to four days.

LAHEM MESHWI
MARINATED LAMB SKEWERS

SERVINGS: 6 | PREP TIME: 10 MINS PLUS MARINATING | COOK TIME: 10 MINS | SKILL LEVEL: 1 (EASY)

INGREDIENTS

1 kg lamb eye round or backstrap
1 cup (250 ml) dry red wine
¼ cup (60 ml) extra virgin
   olive oil
½ tsp dried rosemary
½ tsp dried lemon thyme
   (or regular thyme)
½ tsp dried oregano
½ tsp dried marjoram
½ tsp Aleppo pepper
   or chilli flakes
2 tsp seven-spice mix or
   baharat (mixed spices)
2 tsp salt flakes
hummus and tabouli to serve

METHOD

Trim the lamb of fat and cut into 1½ cm cubes. Place the lamb cubes in a bowl with the wine, olive oil, herbs, spices and salt, and toss well to coat. Cover and marinate in the fridge for a minimum of 2 hours, preferably overnight.

You will need about 12 bamboo skewers, about 20 cm in length, for the lamb. Soak the skewers in water.

Thread about 5 cubes onto each skewer, leaving at least 3 cm free at the bottom and at least a 1 cm gap at the top. This is essentially to make the skewers easier to handle and to encourage even cooking.

Pre-heat the barbecue and cook the skewers to your liking. For medium, cook them on three sides for only 2–3 minutes each side, depending on the strength of the heat. Test one of the pieces of lamb to see if it needs any further cooking.

Serve immediately with hummus and tabouli (see recipes above) and Middle Eastern or your choice of fresh bread.

Spanish food comes from poverty – these dishes are a perfect example of that. This tortilla was always on the table as I was growing up, and pretty much always on my table in our house now. Just 3 ingredients make such a luscious dish and this is the way mum taught me to make it.

FRANK.

MELBOURNE, VIC

TORTILLA DE PATATAS
SPANISH OMELETTE

SERVINGS: 4–6 | PREP TIME: 30 MINS | COOK TIME: 10 MINS | SKILL LEVEL: 2 (MODERATE)

INGREDIENTS

1.2 kg Désirée potatoes
1 litre olive oil, for cooking
1 large brown onion
12 large eggs
60 ml pure olive oil,
  for frying

METHOD

Peel the potatoes and cut into 1 cm cubes, and dice onion. Heat the olive oil in a wide, deep heavy-bottomed pan over a medium heat until just warm, then add the potatoes and onions. Cook on a low to medium heat for 20 minutes. The oil should be just gently bubbling away, but not frying. When done, the potatoes will be soft but should not have gained any colour.

Break the eggs into a bowl and beat with a teaspoon of salt.

Drain the potatoes and onions, and season with salt. Allow to cool a little, then add to the eggs. Gently mix together.

In a 27 cm non-stick frying pan, heat pure olive oil over a high heat. When very hot, pour in the potato and egg mixture and mix well with a heatproof plastic spatula for 30 seconds.

Reduce heat to medium. Use the end of your spatula to break the potatoes up a little. Run the spatula around the side of the tortilla to form the edges. Cook for 3–4 minutes.

Cover the entire pan with a large plate and turn the tortilla over, then slide the uncooked side back into the hot pan. Keep cooking for 3–4 minutes on medium heat, with the plate acting as a lid.

The tortilla should be only lightly browned, and almost cooked through but slightly soft and moist in the centre. Once cooked, remove the plate that was acting as a lid. Place a clean plate on top that fits generously over the pan, then turn the pan over so that the tortilla sits on the plate. Cover with plastic wrap for 15 minutes to allow the latent heat to finish the cooking.

Slice and serve.

SALMOREJO
CHILLED TOMATO & BREAD SOUP

SERVINGS: 6 | PREP TIME: 15 MINS | SKILL LEVEL: 1 (EASY)

INGREDIENTS

1 kg ripe tomatoes
200 g two-day-old rustic
  bread, e.g. pasta dura
1 clove garlic
125 ml extra virgin olive oil
10 g (2 tsp) salt
whites of 3 hard-boiled
  eggs, chopped
100 g serrano ham,
  chopped
olive oil, for drizzling

METHOD

Wash the tomatoes, and roughly chop. Place in a blender and blend to a smooth purée. Pour the purée through a fine sieve over a bowl to remove the seeds and skin, and discard those. Return the purée to the blender.

Break the bread into small pieces, into the blender. Peel and chop the garlic and add to the blender. Add the olive oil and season with the salt. Blend to a smooth purée.

To serve, pour into bowls, decorate with egg and ham, and a drizzle of olive oil.

BAROSSA VALLEY,
SA

MAGGIE BEER AM

CHOCOLATE, QUINCE & ALMOND TART

I've loved quinces for 42 years, from the moment I came to live in the Valley from New South Wales where I was a city girl, and with every farmhouse I ever visited in the Barossa, looking for what we wanted to buy ourselves, there was always a quince tree. Sometimes the cottages were derelict but the quince tree would survive. We planted our first quince orchard nearly 30 years ago and we're still planting quinces now — that's how much I love them.

Maggie

CHOCOLATE, QUINCE & ALMOND TART

SERVINGS: 10–12 | PREP TIME: 50 MINS | COOK TIME: 3¾–4 HOURS | SKILL LEVEL: 2 (MODERATE)

INGREDIENTS

Pot-roasted quinces

500 g quinces, peeled, cored and cut into large wedges

squeeze of lemon juice

250 ml water

150 ml verjuice (plus an extra 100 ml if needed)

140 g caster sugar

Chocolate and almond cream

90 g unsalted butter, softened

110 g caster sugar

2 free-range eggs

1 free-range egg yolk

40 g dark chocolate cocoa

60 ml vino cotto

150 g ground almond meal

To finish

1 x 300 g packet Carême dark chocolate shortcrust pastry

crème fraîche or mascarpone, to serve

METHOD

Pre-heat a fan-forced oven to 170°C (or 190°C for non-fan-forced).

As you peel and core the quinces, place then in a pot of water with the squeeze of lemon juice. This will help stop them oxidising.

To pot-roast the quinces, place the quinces, 250 ml of water, verjuice and caster sugar in a medium-sized heavy-based ovenproof pot. Place this over a high heat and bring to the boil, cover with a lid and place in the oven. Cook for 1 hour, then remove the lid and give the quinces a very light toss, making sure not to break up the wedges.

Place back in the oven and cook for another 1–1½ hours. Check the quinces every 15–20 minutes to make sure that the liquid has not all evaporated; if it starts to, and they look like they will catch on the bottom, add an extra 100 ml of verjuice.

Once the quinces are cooked they should be a beautiful ruby-red colour with a small amount of syrup in the base of the pot. They should not be dry or caught on the base of the pot. Remove the quinces and place on a plate or tray to cool.

Increase the oven temperature to 200°C (220°C non-fan-forced).

To make the chocolate and almond cream, place the butter and caster sugar in a food mixer and beat on high until light and creamy (approximately 6 minutes). With the mixer still running, add the eggs and yolk (one at a time), then the cocoa and vino cotto and mix for a further minute. Add the almond meal and mix until well combined. Set aside until ready to use.

To finish, grease a flan tin (24 cm x 2½ cm) and line with the pastry. Cut off the excess pastry around the edge but allow the pastry to come above the tin by 5 mm, to allow for shrinkage during blind-baking. Place in the fridge for 15 minutes to chill.

Remove the chilled tart shell from the fridge, spike the bottom with a fork, line the top with non-stick baking paper and place blind-baking beans on top (ordinary dried beans or rice work just as well). Bake for 15 minutes, then remove the beans and paper and cook for a further 5 minutes.

Remove the tart shell and reduce the oven temperature to 175°C (195°C non-fan-forced).

Place a third of the chocolate and almond cream on the base of the tart shell. Top with cooked quince wedges and dot the remaining chocolate and almond cream on top. Return the tart to the oven for 50–60 minutes; this time will depend on your oven, but you need to make sure that the chocolate and almond cream is cooked in the centre.

Remove from the oven and allow to cool. Serve with crème fraîche or mascarpone.

There really is nothing better than sitting with family and friends around a table groaning with food and just eating. Or, 'fressing', as we like to say, which is Yiddish for 'eating with abandon'. You don't need to be Jewish, or wait for a special occasion, to enjoy these recipes; they really are the best!

— the Monday Morning Cooking Club

VAUCLUSE, NSW

MONDAY MORNING COOKING CLUB

SARA'S PICKLED BRISKET
GINA'S HAIR-RAISING HONEY CAKE

SARA'S PICKLED BRISKET

SERVINGS: 10–12 | PREP TIME: 20 MINS | COOK TIME: 2¾ HOURS | SKILL LEVEL: 1 (EASY)

INGREDIENTS

1 pickled (corned)
  beef brisket

250 ml (1 cup)
  white vinegar

220 g (1 cup) raw
  or white sugar

9 bay leaves

small handful black
  peppercorns

4 large brown onions,
  halved and sliced

4 tbsp vegetable oil

4 cloves garlic, crushed

250–300 g liquid honey

(DF) (GF)

METHOD

Put the brisket in a large saucepan and cover with water. Add the vinegar and sugar, then bring to the boil, skimming any scum off the surface. Taste to check you have an equal and strong flavour of both vinegar and sugar, and adjust if necessary. Add the bay leaves and peppercorns. Cover the pan with a lid and simmer rapidly for about 2 hours, or until fork-tender.

While the brisket is cooking, gently pan-fry the onions in 2 tablespoons of oil until just starting to brown, about 15 minutes. Set aside.

Pre-heat the oven to 175°C. When the brisket is tender, drain and place it in a non-stick roasting tin. Rub the garlic over the meat and top with the fried onions. Pour the honey over and drizzle with the remaining oil. Roast, uncovered, for about 45 minutes, basting frequently, until the meat is tender and the onions are dark golden.

Slice thickly across the grain and serve warm with mashed potatoes and cabbage, or in a sandwich on fresh rye bread with mustard, pickled cucumber and coleslaw.

GINA'S HAIR-RAISING HONEY CAKE

SERVINGS: 12 | PREP TIME: 12 MINS | COOK TIME: 1 HOUR | SKILL LEVEL: 1 (EASY)

INGREDIENTS

25 g (¼ cup) dry breadcrumbs
375 ml (1½ cups) hot tap water

Dry mixture
225 g (1½ cups) plain flour
225 g (1½ cups) self-raising flour
1½ tsp bicarbonate of soda
40 g (⅓ cup) cocoa powder

Wet mixture
4 eggs
345 g (1½ cups) caster sugar
185 ml (¾ cup) vegetable oil
500 g liquid honey
½ tsp vanilla extract (approx.)

METHOD

Pre-heat the oven to 180°C.

Grease a 26 cm x 10 cm angel cake tin. It is best to use a tin without a removable base, as the mixture is liquid and may leak out. Sprinkle the base and sides of the tin with breadcrumbs, tipping out any excess.

For the dry mixture, sift the dry ingredients together into a bowl. For the wet mixture, in a separate large bowl (or electric mixer bowl), mix the wet ingredients together until well combined. Mix the dry mixture into the wet mixture, alternating with the hot water.

Pour into the prepared cake tin. Bake for 1 hour, or until a skewer inserted into the cake comes out clean. Allow the cake to cool before turning out of the tin.

COLIN FASSNIDGE
FOUR IN HAND

SALAD OF WATERMELON, FENNEL, PEAS & FETA
LAMB STEW WITH TOMATO & OLIVES

Our trick at home with feeding the kids is to find out what they like thats healthy — then we just pound it into them! ☺

MATRAVILLE, NSW

SALAD OF WATERMELON, FENNEL, PEAS & FETA

SERVINGS: 4 | PREP TIME: 15 MINS | SKILL LEVEL: 1 (EASY)

INGREDIENTS

½ large watermelon

2 baby fennel

1 cup creamy-style feta

1 cup shelled garden peas
  (defrosted baby peas
  also work)

½ bunch mint,
  leaves picked

good-quality olive oil

salt and pepper

GF V

METHOD

Cut watermelon flesh into bite-sized chunks. Shave or finely slice the fennel, and gently crumble the feta.

In a salad bowl, combine the watermelon, fennel, feta, peas and mint. Dress with a drizzle of olive oil and salt and pepper to taste.

LAMB STEW WITH TOMATO & OLIVES

SERVINGS: 4–6 | PREP TIME: 40 MINS | COOK TIME: 8 HOURS OR OVERNIGHT
SKILL LEVEL: 1 (EASY)

INGREDIENTS

1 kg lamb shoulder,
  bone in

olive oil

1 carrot, peeled and
  roughly chopped

1 large brown onion,
  peeled and roughly
  chopped

3 stalks celery, peeled
  and roughly chopped

1 bay leaf (fresh is best)

¼ bunch thyme

¼ bunch rosemary

1 x 400 g can chopped
  tomatoes

1 cup pitted large
  green olives

4 cups chicken stock,
  warmed

salt and pepper

knob of butter

GF

METHOD

Pre-heat the oven to 90°C. Heat a large ovenproof pot (large enough to fit the lamb shoulder in) on the stove on a medium to high heat. Coat the lamb shoulder in a little olive oil and brown it on both sides. Remove the lamb and set aside.

Add the carrot, onion and celery, as well as the bay leaf, thyme and rosemary, to the pot and sauté the vegetables and herbs until the onion is translucent and has taken on a little colour. Add the lamb back to the pot, along with the canned tomatoes, the olives and enough chicken stock to submerge the shoulder by about three-quarters. Season with salt and pepper and bring the braising liquid to the boil. Once boiling, cover the pot with a tight-fitting lid, or tinfoil, and carefully transfer it to the oven. Allow the lamb to cook low and slow overnight, or for at least 8 hours.

To serve, remove the lamb from the oven, remove the lid or tinfoil, and carefully lift out the lamb. Remove the large flat bone from the shoulder and discard. Place the pot on the stovetop and bring the braising liquid to the boil. Discard any twigs of thyme and rosemary and reduce the liquid by half. Add the butter and whisk to combine. Gently tear up the lamb into chunks and place them back in the braising liquid. Season to taste and serve with salad or mashed potatoes and blanched baby vegetables.

SPENCER PATRICK
HARRISONS

ASIAN CHILLI MUD CRAB
PINEAPPLE & COCONUT CRUMBLE

Everything I've cooked here comes from my surrounds. The mud crabs come from the mangroves in the back garden, pineapples from a local grower, and coconuts that fell onto the ground in my front yard. I love living in Far North Queensland;
This is my paradise.
- Spencer

PORT DOUGLAS, QLD

ASIAN CHILLI MUD CRAB

SERVINGS: 2 | PREP TIME: 3 MINS PLUS MARINATING | COOK TIME: 25 MINS | SKILL LEVEL: 1 (EASY)

INGREDIENTS

2 brown onions
6 red chillies (hot ones)
100 ml vegetable oil
200 ml tomato paste
60 ml kecap manis
2 tbsp white vinegar
200 g ginger

3 sticks lemongrass, chopped
4 kaffir lime leaves
1 large mud crab

Garnish
½ bunch coriander
½ bunch Thai basil
2 limes

(DF)

METHOD

Place all ingredients (except crab, of course) into a food processor and blend, seasoning with salt and pepper to taste. Toss with crab and leave for 2 hours. You can give the thicker parts of the crab shell and claws a few good blows with a mallet to crack the shell and allow the marinade in. It also makes it easier to eat later.

Heat a wok to hot and add marinated crab. Toss and cook until shell turns orange and flesh is translucent – approximately 25 minutes. If the wok gets too dry, add a splash of sea water or beer of your choice.

Place in serving bowl and garnish with scattered herbs and wedges of lime.

PINEAPPLE & COCONUT CRUMBLE

SERVINGS: 4 | PREP TIME: 30 MINS | SKILL LEVEL: 2 (MODERATE)

INGREDIENTS

Pineapple
1 medium ripe pineapple
250 g coconut sugar
  (available in health
  food stores and in
  the organics section
  of some supermarkets)
250 ml dark rum
cracked pepper to taste

Sago
75 g sago
400 ml coconut milk
150 g coconut sugar
zest and juice of 1 lime

Crumble
½ packet Gingernut
  biscuits
handful shredded coconut

White chocolate snow
35 g white chocolate
75 g maltodextrin

METHOD

Peel pineapple and dice evenly. Place pineapple and coconut sugar in a frying pan and heat until caramelised. Add rum and pepper – be careful, there will be flames! Reduce by half until a syrup has formed, then remove from the heat.

Place sago and coconut milk in a saucepan and cook on a slow heat until sago pearls become transparent; this should take approximately 20 minutes. Add sugar and lime zest and juice, cook until sugar and lime is incorporated and then remove from the heat.

Crush Gingernut biscuits to a crumble consistency in a food processor. Toast coconut lightly in a dry frying pan and allow to cool. Mix Gingernut crumble and coconut together.

Melt chocolate in a double boiler or in a small heatproof bowl set over a pan of simmering water, and place in a food processor. Add maltodextrin, while blending, until the mixture forms a snow.

To assemble, pour sago into four small glass serving bowls, then top with pineapple and syrup. Sprinkle on the crumble, and finish with snow.

ANNA POLYVIOU
SHANGRI-LA HOTEL

SUMMER TRIFLE WITH TROPICAL FRUITS

I LOVE BEING A PASTRY CHEF, WE'RE ALWAYS HAPPY BECAUSE WE GET TO SPEND ALL DAY MAKING DESSERT! LET'S FACE IT, NOBODY REMEMBERS THEIR ENTRÈE OR MAIN; ITS ALWAYS DESSERT THAT LEAVES THE LASTING IMPRESSION OF A MEAL!

ANNA POLYVIOU :)

THE ROCKS, NSW

SUMMER TRIFLE WITH TROPICAL FRUITS

SERVINGS: 12–14 | PREP TIME: 1 HOUR | COOK TIME: 4 HOURS PLUS COOLING
SKILL LEVEL: 2 (MODERATE)

INGREDIENTS

Pavlova
100 g egg whites
  (from about 4 eggs)
100 g caster sugar
100 g icing sugar

*Mango and
passionfruit jelly*
50 g gelatine sheets
700 ml passionfruit purée
150 g caster sugar
800 ml mango purée

Pastry cream
1 litre milk
seeds of 1 vanilla pod
240 g egg yolks (from
  about 12 eggs)
250 g caster sugar
95 g cornflour
100 g unsalted butter,
  softened

Diplomat cream
750 g pastry cream
375 ml cream

Tropical compote
1 pineapple
2 mangoes
pulp of 5 passionfruit
100 g mango popping
  pearls (aka boba,
  bursting tapioca balls
  used in Asian bubble teas)

Garnish
1 punnet baby
  coriander leaves

METHOD

Pavlova: pre-heat the oven to 140°C. Line two baking trays with non-stick baking paper. Using an electric mixer with a whisk attachment, whisk egg whites with caster sugar, to firm-peak stage. Remove the whisk attachment and gradually fold in icing sugar.

Using a plain nozzle, pipe 100 g of the mixture into meringue kisses on one of the trays. Place the rest of the meringue mix in large spoonfuls onto the other tray (use a salad spoon).

Bake large meringues for 4 hours and kisses for 1 hour 15 minutes. Turn off the oven and allow meringues to cool for 1–2 hours. Do not open the door until the oven has completely cooled.

Jelly: soften gelatine sheets in ice water for a few minutes. In a small saucepan, warm passionfruit purée and caster sugar together, until sugar is dissolved and purée is hot (but not boiled). Remove from the heat, whisk in softened gelatine sheets, add mango purée and strain. Pour into a 20 cm glass trifle bowl and allow to set.

Pastry cream: in a medium saucepan, bring milk and vanilla seeds to the boil. Meanwhile, whisk egg yolks and sugar together, and stir cornflour in.

When milk has boiled, take it off the heat and pour a little into the egg mixture. Whisk and return to the pan. Place back on the heat and whisk until the pastry cream is thick, 5–8 minutes.

Remove from the heat, put into an electric mixer with a paddle attachment and beat until cool. When cooled to 40°C, gradually add in the butter.

Diplomat cream: whisk the pastry cream until smooth and lump free. Reduce the speed, and add in the cream until the mixture is soft and semi-whisked.

Tropical compote: peel pineapple and mango and cut flesh into 2 cm cubes. Add passionfruit pulp and mango pearls and mix together.

To assemble, once jelly is set, break the spooned meringue on top of the jelly. Spoon the diplomat cream over the meringue, then tropical fruit compote on top, followed by meringue kisses and baby coriander.

MUDGEE,
NSW

KIM CURRIE
THE ZIN HOUSE

**CONTENTS OF FRIDGE &
GARDEN PASTA**

**KIM'S NEAPOLITAN
ICE-CREAM CAKE**

I wonder if my mother didn't have an Italian lover somewhere - our family are obsessed with pasta! It's the best food; so simple and satisfying. As long as you have pasta in the pantry and a few ingredients, you can create a delicious meal that everyone can share. *Kim Currie*

CONTENTS OF FRIDGE & GARDEN PASTA

SERVINGS: 4 | PREP TIME: 20 MINS | SKILL LEVEL: 1 (EASY)

INGREDIENTS

1 packet good-quality
  pasta or 500 g
  home-made

4 or 5 rashers streaky
  bacon, rind removed,
  roughly chopped
  (salami or prosciutto
  is also good)

several cloves garlic,
  peeled and sliced

1 large brown onion,
  peeled and roughly
  chopped

chopped fresh chilli to taste

handful of fresh herbs
  to taste (rosemary and
  thyme work well)

good-quality olive oil

approx. 500 g tomatoes,
  chopped (or 1 x 400 g
  can chopped tomatoes)

approx. 500 g greens from
  the garden or the fridge
  (spinach leaves, rocket,
  zucchini or whatever
  you have to hand)

2 free-range eggs

chopped fresh parsley,
  to serve

salt and pepper

freshly grated Parmesan,
  to serve

METHOD

The principle of this dish is to use what is to hand and what is in season, so these ingredients are a guide only. The idea is to use whatever you find in the garden or fridge that you like, and throw it in. If you don't like something in this recipe, don't put it in! The eggs added in at the end help to 'set' the pasta, and cook in the warmth of the pasta on the way to the table.

In a large pot of boiling, salted water, cook the pasta – 'just' (it will continue to cook in the pan, so aim for it to be slightly underdone). While the pasta is cooking, make the sauce. Sauté the bacon, garlic, onion, chilli and fresh herbs in a little olive oil in a large pan or wok on a medium to high heat. When the onion is translucent and the bacon has taken on some colour, add the tomatoes and let the liquid reduce a bit. You could add a little stock or wine if you like, but it's not necessary. Stir through the chopped garden greens and allow everything to combine for a minute or two. Remove the pan from the heat and set aside to cool slightly.

Drain the nearly-done pasta and refresh it in a little cold water. Once drained, add the pasta to the pan or wok with the sauce, crack the eggs in and give everything a good stir. You can pile this onto a serving platter, but we usually just take the pan to the table. Finish the dish with a scattering of freshly chopped parsley, a drizzle of olive oil and a generous amount of salt and pepper. Serve the pasta with some freshly grated Parmesan, optional extra olive oil and more freshly chopped chillies and get everyone to help themselves.

KIM'S NEAPOLITAN ICE-CREAM CAKE

SERVINGS: 12 | PREP TIME: 30 MINS PLUS COOLING, CHURNING & FREEZING
SKILL LEVEL: 2 (MODERATE)

INGREDIENTS

1 cup espresso coffee
½ cup Dutch cocoa
¾ cup caster or icing sugar
1 packet sponge or
  Savoiardi finger biscuits
  (about 400 g)
1 batch honey ice-cream
  (recipe below)
300 g raspberries puréed
  with 1 cup sugar
1 cup whole raspberries
  (fresh are best, but frozen
  will work well, too)

Honey ice-cream
8 egg yolks
100 g sugar
100 g honey
800 ml cream
1 vanilla bean, split

METHOD

First, make the honey ice-cream: whisk the eggs yolks, sugar and honey together until thick.

Put the cream and split vanilla bean in a thick-bottomed pan and bring to the boil.

Whisk in the egg mix and stir continuously over a low heat until the mixture coats the back of a wooden spoon. Pass through a fine strainer and allow to cool.

Now make a syrup by combining the coffee, cocoa and sugar.

Pour this over the sponge biscuits and toss to coat evenly. Leave to soak up any extra liquid.

Divide the ice-cream base into two. Churn one half as is, and the second half with the puréed raspberries. (You could divide it into three and add melted chocolate to the third for another layer.)

Line a pudding or mixing bowl with baking paper. Cover the base and sides with the soaked biscuits.

Add a layer of about two-thirds of the honey ice-cream over the biscuits, top with the raspberry ice-cream and then sprinkle with the whole raspberries. Then add the last of the honey ice-cream and finally finish with a layer of the biscuits.

Cover with baking paper, push down gently to ensure a smooth fit between the layers, and freeze until completely set.

Serve with whatever fresh fruit is in season – cherries are particularly good in summer.

KYLIE KWONG

STIR-FRIED HOKKIEN NOODLES WITH CHICKEN, CHILLI & BEAN SPROUTS

These days, a wok is as common in an Australian home as a barbecue and a fry pan. And I just love stir-frying because of the way the high heat cooks food so quickly and beautifully with all those caramelly flavours and so on. It's so accessible and simple.

Kylie

POTTS POINT, NSW

STIR-FRIED HOKKIEN NOODLES WITH CHICKEN, CHILLI & BEAN SPROUTS

SERVINGS: 4 | PREP TIME: 30 MINS | COOK TIME: 8 MINS | SKILL LEVEL: 1 (EASY)

INGREDIENTS

400 g chicken thigh fillets,
  cut into 2 cm slices
¼ cup vegetable oil
1 small white onion,
  cut in half and then
  into thick wedges
12 slices fresh ginger
1 x 450 g packet fresh
  Hokkien noodles
2 tbsp Shaoxing wine
  or dry sherry

1 tbsp white sugar
2 tbsp light soy sauce
1 tbsp malt vinegar
½ tsp sesame oil
1 cup fresh bean sprouts
½ cup julienned
  spring onion
2 large red chillies, finely sliced
  on the diagonal

Marinade
1 tbsp white sugar
1 tbsp light soy sauce
1 tbsp Shaoxing wine
  or dry sherry
½ tsp sesame oil

METHOD

Combine the chicken with marinade ingredients in a bowl, cover, and leave to marinate in the fridge for 30 minutes.

Heat 2 tablespoons of the oil in a hot wok until the surface seems to shimmer slightly. Add chicken and stir-fry for 1 minute. Remove from wok and set aside.

Add remaining oil to hot wok with onion and ginger, and stir-fry for 1 minute or until onion is lightly browned. Toss in noodles, reserved chicken, wine or sherry, sugar, soy sauce, vinegar and sesame oil, and stir-fry for 1½ minutes. Add bean sprouts, spring onion and half the chilli, and stir-fry for a further 30 seconds or until chicken is just cooked through and the noodles are hot.

Arrange noodles in bowls, top with remaining chilli and serve immediately.

FREMANTLE, WA

JIM MENDOLIA
FREMANTLE SARDINES

———————————

MUM'S FRIED SARDINES
WITH HERBED MAYONNAISE
BARBECUED SARDINES

I was brought up in an Italian fishing family and just love it. Every morning we get up before dawn to chase sardines. The dolphins come out, we watch the sunrise; there's really nothing like it. Jim

MUM'S FRIED SARDINES WITH HERBED MAYONNAISE

SERVINGS: 6 | PREP TIME: | COOK TIME: | SKILL LEVEL: 1 (EASY)

INGREDIENTS

4 cups fresh breadcrumbs

¾ cup grated Parmesan

2 tbsp chopped parsley,
  plus extra for garnish

24 sardines, cleaned and
  boned linguetta fashion
  (butterfly-style fillet; can be
  bought ready-prepared)

1 cup plain flour

2 eggs

4 tbsp milk

olive oil for frying

lemon wedges to serve

Herbed mayonnaise

¾ cup good-quality
  mayonnaise

1 tbsp chopped parsley

1 finely chopped shallot

3 tsp chopped capers

1 tbsp chopped gherkins

METHOD

Herbed mayonnaise: combine all the ingredients, mixing well and seasoning with salt and freshly ground black pepper.

Sardines: combine breadcrumbs, Parmesan, parsley, and salt and freshly ground black pepper to taste. Place in a wide, shallow bowl.

Place flour in another wide, shallow bowl. Beat eggs with milk in a third wide, shallow bowl.

Open sardines flat and coat lightly with flour, dip in combined egg and milk, then coat well with breadcrumb mixture.

Heat oil in a frying pan and cook sardines on both sides until golden-brown and cooked through – approximately 2 minutes each side.

Serve hot with herbed mayonnaise and lemon wedges. Garnish with extra parsley.

BARBECUED SARDINES

SERVINGS: 6 | PREP TIME: 25 MINS | COOK TIME: 4 MINS | SKILL LEVEL: 1 (EASY)

INGREDIENTS

24 fresh sardines

Dressing

1 cup good olive oil

¼ cup water

2 cloves garlic

1 tbsp dried
  oregano leaves

2 tbsp chopped
  fresh parsley

1 long red chilli, sliced

(DF) (GF)

METHOD

Remove guts from sardines and wash clean in cold water. Sardines can be prepared several hours ahead; store them, covered, in the fridge.

Combine all dressing ingredients and place in a shallow dish.

Pre-heat hot-plate or grill and brush with a little oil. Place sardines on top, lightly sprinkle fish with salt and brush well with dressing. Turn occasionally. When sardines have been turned for the first time, sprinkle with more salt and brush more dressing on the exposed side.

The cooking time will vary according to the heat of the hot-plate or grill; generally fish is cooked when it comes away easily from the backbone. It should take about 2 minutes for each side. Keep a regular check, basting with extra dressing as needed.

If desired, serve any remaining dressing alongside the fish to dip in for additional flavour.

This Korean Chicken Soup became a family favourite to cook on Sunday nights at home, and sometimes I like to make it at Quay. When you have a really stressful, busy day, the staff meal is something that everyone looks forward to, and something comforting like this soup give you ten minutes out of your day. For me, it makes me feel like I'm home and then we get back into work.

Peter Gilmore

PETER GILMORE
QUAY

KOREAN CHICKEN SOUP

THE ROCKS,
NSW

KOREAN CHICKEN SOUP

SERVINGS: 6 | PREP TIME: 30 MINS | COOK TIME: 1½ HOURS | SKILL LEVEL: 1 (EASY)

INGREDIENTS

1.8 kg whole
  free-range chicken

2.5 litres cold water

100 g unsalted butter

2 tbsp Korean sesame oil

2 medium onions,
  roughly diced

1 small knob fresh ginger,
  finely sliced

3 cloves garlic, finely diced

100 g fresh shiitake
  mushrooms, finely sliced

150 g fresh oyster
  mushrooms,
  torn into thirds

3 tsp mild Korean
  chilli flakes

2 tbsp fish sauce

2 tbsp light soy sauce

300 g chopped kimchi
  (available from Asian
  supermarkets)

400 g thin somen
  wheat noodles

1 small bunch baby bok
  choy, finely sliced

5 Asian green spring
  onions, white part only,
  finely sliced

2 tbsp fresh lime juice

fine sea salt to taste

2 free-range eggs, beaten

3 tbsp toasted
  sesame seeds, for garnish

METHOD

Place the chicken in a large saucepan with the cold water. Bring the chicken and the water just to boiling point, then reduce to a low simmer for 30 minutes. Carefully remove the chicken with a pair of tongs and a spoon and place into a colander. Allow the chicken to cool for 15 minutes.

Wearing gloves, remove the leg, thigh and breast meat. Return all the chicken bones and carcass to the cooking liquid and continue to simmer on low for a further 30 minutes. Chop the cooled chicken meat into small pieces and place in the refrigerator.

To a separate clean saucepan, add the butter and sesame oil and place on a medium heat. Add the onion and sweat for 2 minutes. Add the ginger and garlic and sweat for a further minute. Add the shiitake and oyster mushrooms and sweat for 2 minutes. Add the chilli flakes, fish sauce, soy sauce and kimchi. Stir and remove from the heat.

Use a ladle to remove any impurities and fat from the surface of the chicken stock. Pass the stock through a fine sieve and add it to the pan of vegetables. Simmer soup on low for 20 minutes.

Bring a separate pan of water to the boil, add the somen noodles and cook for 2 minutes. Drain the noodles and divide equally between six warmed bowls. Turn the soup up to high, add the chicken meat, bok choy, spring onions and lime juice. As soon as the soup starts to boil, turn off the heat. Taste the soup and correct the seasoning with sea salt if necessary. Stir the soup to create a whirlpool, then add the beaten egg. Serve a generous ladleful of soup on top of the warm noodles and garnish with toasted sesame seeds.

ROSS O'MEARA
BRUNY ISLAND FOOD

TWICE-COOKED WALLABY SHANKS
WITH SALSA VERDE
SLOW-ROASTED PORK SHOULDER

It's important to me that my kids have a sense of direct contact with their food. We run pigs, commercially shoot wallaby and make our own produce from it. It's a bit funny when my four year old picks up a snag from a sausage sizzle and says "I can't eat this, It's not my dad's." But it makes me thankful they appreciate food that's had very little done to it.

Ross

BRUNY ISLAND, TAS

TWICE-COOKED WALLABY SHANKS
WITH SALSA VERDE

SERVINGS: 4 | PREP TIME: 45 MINS | COOK TIME: 25 MINS | SKILL LEVEL: 1 (EASY)

INGREDIENTS

8 wallaby shanks
300 ml chicken stock
20 ml oil for cooking

Salsa verde
1 handful basil
1 handful flat-leaf parsley
1 handful spring onions
1 small handful chives
3 cloves purple garlic
3 tsp baby capers, rinsed
5 anchovy fillets
juice from 2 lemons
200 ml extra virgin olive oil

METHOD

Place the shanks in a saucepan deep enough to allow you to cover them with stock. Place the shanks and stock over a high heat and bring to the boil. Once boiling, turn down to a rolling simmer and cook for 30 minutes. Take the shanks off the heat and let them cool down in the cooking liquid. (If you don't have time, you can take them out of the stock and leave them to cool down.)

Place the herbs, garlic, capers, anchovies and lemon juice in a blender or food processor. Start on a low speed, and add the olive oil slowly while increasing the speed. Keep the machine going until the mix forms a nice smooth paste, adding salt and pepper to taste. Spoon the paste into a serving bowl, ready for the shanks.

Take a good-sized frying pan, big enough to fit the shanks, and place it over a high heat. If you have a good barbecue or can cook over coals, these shanks are great cooked that way. Put a little oil in the pan before placing the shanks down or, if barbecuing, rub the oil on the shanks before you place them down. The shanks will already be cooked, so you are just crisping them up. So, slowly turn them for 15 minutes.

Once they are done, place them on a platter and top with the salsa verde.

SLOW-ROASTED PORK SHOULDER

SERVINGS: 8 | PREP TIME: 15 MINS | COOK TIME: 6 HOURS | SKILL LEVEL: 1 (EASY)

INGREDIENTS

3 kg free-range pork
  shoulder, bone out
  and skin on

olive oil and salt
  for cooking

1 kg waxy potatoes,
  e.g. Pink Fir Apple

3 French shallots,
  peeled and sliced

5 cloves purple garlic,
  peeled and sliced

3 anchovy fillets

1 handful chopped chives

1 handful chopped
  flat-leaf parsley

100 ml chicken stock

(DF) (GF)

METHOD

Pre-heat the oven to 150°C (if it's fan-forced, turn it down to 130°C). Take your pork shoulder and rub it dry with paper towel, then rub the top with oil and salt and leave it to the side. Wash the potatoes and cut into slices about ¾ cm thick.

Get a large, deep roasting dish and add the sliced potatoes, shallots, garlic, anchovies and herbs. Mix all the ingredients up and then make sure they are evenly spread. Add the stock and place the pork on top. Place the dish into the oven and cook for 6 hours.

Check the pork after 2–3 hours to see that it is not cooking too quickly. If the skin has coloured and crisped, place a piece of tinfoil over the top and continue cooking. If the crackle isn't working, heat up your grill and once it is hot slide your pork under. Be very careful as it will burn very quickly – make sure you are there watching it at all times.

Serve with cooked greens or salads.

I love butter and sugar; I could just eat butter sugar, whipped up or cooked in a pan. And the smell of it! My grandfather used to make pikelets for us and they were always beautiful and fluffy, and now when I smell the butter in the pan, waiting for the batter to be dropped in, I always think of him.
Phillippa

PRAHRAN
VIC

PANELA PIKELETS

MAKES: APPROX. 24 | PREP TIME: 10 MINS | COOK TIME: 12–15 MINS | SKILL LEVEL: 1 (EASY)

INGREDIENTS

150 g stoneground flour
(or plain white flour if you
can't find stoneground)

1 tsp baking powder

1 egg, at room
temperature

60 g panela sugar
(unrefined cane sugar)

180 ml milk

30 g melted butter, plus
extra butter for cooking

icing sugar and butter,
or mango/raspberry jam
and cream, to serve

METHOD

Blend together the flour and baking powder with a whisk until evenly combined.

Ideally using an electric hand-held beater, whisk together the egg and sugar until thick and pale. Mix the milk into the melted butter and blend into the egg mixture.

Gently fold the flour into the eggs a third at a time, being careful not to knock too much air out of the eggs. The batter will become rubbery if it is over-mixed.

Heat a heavy-based frying pan to medium hot. Drop a small piece of butter into the pan, swirl it around to coat the entire surface and let it burn. Remove all residue with paper towel. Use a dessertspoon to drop spoonfuls of batter into the pan. When small holes appear on the surface of the batter, usually after about 1½ minutes, they should be ready to turn over. They should be golden on the base. Cook for a further minute, then remove to a plate and cover with a clean tea towel to keep them warm.

Continue cooking until the batter has all been used, spreading a little more butter lightly around the base of the pan, as needed, to keep the pikelets from sticking. Serve with butter and a dusting of icing sugar, or jam and cream. They make a great picnic or lunch-box snack.

CHOCOLATE RASPBERRY BROWNIE

MAKES: 24 PIECES | PREP TIME: 20 MINS | COOK TIME: 45–50 MINS | SKILL LEVEL: 1 (EASY)

INGREDIENTS

200 g cultured butter

350 g chocolate
(55% cocoa),
cut into 1 cm pieces

430 g caster sugar

4 eggs

1½ tbsp water

1 tsp vanilla extract

pinch of salt

190 g self-raising flour

100 g walnut halves
(optional)

125 g raspberries
(fresh or frozen)

METHOD

Pre-heat oven to 170°C (150°C fan-forced). Line a 20 cm x 30 cm slice tray with non-stick baking paper.

Melt butter and chocolate together in a bowl over simmering water. Remove when almost melted and stir until well blended, then cool until at room temperature.

Stir in sugar, eggs, water and vanilla until well mixed. Fold in salt and flour.

Pour into the prepared tray and spread until an even thickness. Sprinkle evenly with walnuts (if using) and raspberries.

Bake on the centre shelf of oven for 45–50 minutes. There should be a crust on the surface but it should still be a little moist in the centre while hot. It will set when cold. Leave in the tin to cool, then remove to a board to cut.

Store in an airtight container for five days in a cool place, or longer in the fridge.

SEAN McCONNELL
MONSTER KITCHEN & BAR

BLACK BARLEY & WILD RICE SALAD WITH CANDIED ALMONDS, BARBERRY & SHANKLEESH

WOOD-ROASTED PINE MUSHROOMS & SLIPPERY JACKS WITH LOADS OF PARMESAN

I GO OUT EVERY YEAR TO PICK MUSHROOMS. I EVEN GO OUT A MONTH BEFORE THEY'RE READY, JUST TO CHECK. I'M REALLY LOOKING FORWARD TO TAKING MY LITTLE BOY AND MY NEW LITTLE ONE AND PASSING ON THAT KNOWLEDGE. HOPEFULLY THEY'LL GET AS MUCH OF A KICK OUT OF IT AS I DO.

— SEAN

NEWACTON
ACT

BLACK BARLEY & WILD RICE SALAD WITH CANDIED ALMONDS, BARBERRY & SHANKLEESH

SERVINGS: 6 | PREP TIME: 40 MINS | SKILL LEVEL: 2 (MODERATE)

INGREDIENTS

Candied almonds
2 tbsp sugar
splash of rose-water
1 cup slivered almonds

Grains
200 g wild rice
200 g black barley

Puffed rice
50 g wild rice
1 litre (approx.) vegetable
  oil for puffing rice

To serve
2 tbsp dried barberries
2 tbsp sumac
splash of olive oil
zest and juice of 1 lemon
100 g shankleesh
  (Lebanese cheese)
2 tbsp dried rose petals

METHOD

Make the candied almonds: pre-heat the oven to 180°C. Combine the sugar with 2 tablespoons of water and the rose-water and heat gently until the sugar dissolves. Add the almonds to the pan and mix to entirely coat the almonds. Lay the almonds out on a tray lined with baking paper and roast until lightly caramelised (approximately 8 minutes). Set aside.

Cook the grains: to separate saucepans, add 1 litre of cold water and add your wild rice and barley to each pot. Add a pinch of salt and place over a medium heat. Bring to a simmer and cook at a gentle simmer until the grains are cooked through but not falling apart – between 20 and 30 minutes. When the grains are cooked, strain and set aside.

Puff the wild rice: heat the vegetable oil to 200°C. Add the wild rice and cook for about 20 seconds, being very careful as the oil will spit as the grains puff up. Remove the puffed rice and drain on paper towel.

To serve: toss the grains with the almonds, barberries, sumac, olive oil, lemon zest and juice. Season with sea salt and place in a bowl or a large serving dish. Crumble the shankleesh over the top, then sprinkle the rose petals, and finish with the puffed wild rice.

WOOD-ROASTED PINE MUSHROOMS & SLIPPERY JACKS WITH LOADS OF PARMESAN

SERVINGS: 8 | PREP TIME: 15 MINS | COOK TIME: 10 MINS | SKILL LEVEL: 1 (EASY)

INGREDIENTS

1 kg each medium
   pine mushrooms
   and slippery jacks
   (available mid-autumn)

½ cup good-quality
   extra virgin olive oil

5 cloves garlic,
   crushed with the
   back of a large knife

50 g butter

10 sprigs thyme

juice of 2 lemons

100 g Parmesan

handful of
   chopped parsley

METHOD

If you don't have a woodfire oven, pre-heat a domestic oven to 180°C. If you do have a woodfire oven, get it cranking!

Brush any pine needles or grit from the pine mushrooms and slice in half. Peel the skin off the top of the slippery jack caps, brush off any dirt or pine needles and cut in half.

Heat a large, heavy baking tray in the oven until it's piping hot. Then, remove it from the oven, add the olive oil, garlic, butter, mushrooms and thyme, and season with sea salt and freshly ground black pepper.

Return to the oven and cook for about 10 minutes. Remove the mushrooms from the tray and arrange on a large serving dish. Pour the pan juices and lemon juice over. Grate the Parmesan over the top as finely as you can. Scatter the parsley on top and serve.

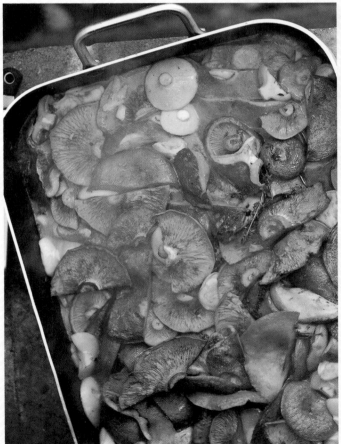

CHARMAINE SOLOMON OAM

LAMPRIES:
GHEE RICE
LAMPRIES CURRY
FRIKKADELS
VAMBOTU PAHI
SEENI SAMBOLA
PRAWN BLACAN

Lampries is an entire Sri Lankan meal in one fragrant parcel, with flavourful rice, chilli sambol, curry and Dutch meat-balls. We served them at my first book launch back in 1972, which sounds like ancient history, doesn't it! I like that my daughters are good cooks because now when I get in the kitchen I have help! — Charmaine

CONCORD, NSW

LAMPRIES
SRI LANKAN CURRY PARCELS

SERVINGS: 16–18 | PREP TIME: 10 MINS | COOK TIME: 25 MINS | SKILL LEVEL: 1 (EASY)

It is practical to make a large number of lampries, as they are ideal for parties. They freeze well and can be kept frozen for two months. Heat in a moderate oven from frozen state for 40 minutes, or 20 minutes if thawed in the fridge. If you are making lampries for a smaller occasion, simply halve all the recipes.

INGREDIENTS

banana leaves

3 quantities Ghee Rice (see below)

1 quantity Lampries Curry (page 95)

1 quantity Frikkadels (page 95)

1 quantity Eggplant Pickle (page 96)

1 quantity Chilli Sambol (page 97)

1 quantity Prawn Blacan (page 97)

1 x 400 ml can thick coconut milk

METHOD

Using large, wide banana leaves, strip them from the centre rib and cut into pieces approximately 30–40 cm long. Wash and dry with a clean tea towel and heat over a gas flame for a few seconds on each side, to make them pliable so they will fold without splitting. Alternatively, put the banana leaves in a large basin or sink and pour boiling water over the top. If you can't get banana leaves, use 40 cm squares of tinfoil instead.

Pre-heat the oven to 190°C.

On each banana leaf, place 1 cup of firmly packed ghee rice and arrange 2 tablespoons of lampries curry, 2 frikkadels, 1 teaspoon of eggplant pickle, 1 teaspoon of chilli sambol and 1 heaped teaspoon of prawn blacan around the rice. Pour 2 tablespoons of thick coconut milk over the rice. Fold the banana leaf over and fasten with short bamboo skewers (or fold the tinfoil over) to make a neat oblong package. Some people like to enclose the leaf parcels in tinfoil as well – this is a good idea, in case the leaf splits while heating or serving.

Heat the lampries in the oven for about 20–25 minutes, then remove and arrange on a large serving tray. When the lampries are opened, the fragrance of the food is unbelievably appetising. Allow 1–2 lampries for each guest.

GHEE RICE

SERVINGS: 4–5 | PREP TIME: 5 MINS PLUS DRAINING
COOK TIME: 20 MINS | SKILL LEVEL: 1 (EASY)

INGREDIENTS

400 g (2 cups) basmati or other long-grain rice

2½ tbsp ghee

1 large onion, thinly sliced

4 cloves

6 cardamom pods, bruised

1 stick cinnamon

875 ml (3½ cups) beef, chicken or mutton stock

2 tsp salt

METHOD

Wash the rice well and drain in a colander for 30 minutes.

Heat the ghee in a saucepan over a medium heat. Add the onion and cook until golden. Add the spices and rice and cook for 5 minutes, stirring constantly with a slotted metal spoon.

Add the hot stock and salt and bring to the boil, then reduce the heat to low, cover, and cook for 15–20 minutes without lifting the lid. Remove from the heat, uncover and rest for 5 minutes to allow steam to escape. Gently fluff up the rice with a fork, removing the whole spices.

When transferring the rice to a serving dish, use a slotted metal spoon to avoid crushing the grains of rice. Serve hot, accompanied by curries of meat and vegetables, pickles and sambols.

LAMPRIES CURRY

SERVINGS: 16–18 | PREP TIME: 25 MINS | COOK TIME: 2¾ HOURS | SKILL LEVEL: 1 (EASY)

INGREDIENTS

500 g chuck steak
500 g diced leg of lamb
  or mutton
5 tsp salt, plus extra to taste
8 cardamom pods
20 whole black peppercorns
500 g chicken thighs
1 tbsp ghee
2 tbsp oil
4 onions, finely chopped

8 garlic cloves, finely chopped
1 tbsp finely chopped
  fresh ginger
2 tsp curry leaves, crushed
¼ tsp fenugreek seeds
  (optional)
4 tbsp Ceylon curry powder
1 tsp ground turmeric
1 tsp chilli powder
1 stick cinnamon

1 tsp ground cardamom
3 pandanus leaves (available
  from Asian grocery stores)
3 stems lemongrass, bruised,
  or 2 strips lemon zest
2 tbsp lemon juice
500 g pork belly, diced
625 ml (2½ cups)
  thick coconut milk

METHOD

Put the steak and lamb or mutton in a large saucepan with enough cold water to cover. Add 2 teaspoons of the salt, the cardamom pods and peppercorns. Cover and simmer for 30 minutes, then add the chicken and simmer for 15 minutes. Allow to cool, then strain and cut all of the meats into very small dice, discarding the bones.

Heat the ghee and oil in a large saucepan over a medium heat. Add the onion, garlic, ginger and curry leaves and cook until the onion is golden. Add the fenugreek seeds, if using, and cook for 1 minute, then add the curry powder, turmeric, chilli, cinnamon, cardamom, pandanus leaves, lemongrass, remaining salt, lemon juice, diced pork and half the coconut milk. Stir well, cover, and cook over a low heat for 30 minutes.

Return the other meats to the pan, add the remaining coconut milk and simmer, uncovered, for 1½ hours, or until the meat is tender and the sauce has thickened. Serve hot.

FRIKKADELS
DUTCH FORCEMEAT BALLS

MAKES: APPROX. 40 | PREP TIME: 10 MINS | COOK TIME: 20 MINS | SKILL LEVEL: 1 (EASY)

INGREDIENTS

1 tbsp butter
1 small onion, finely chopped
500 g minced beef
30 g (½ cup) fresh breadcrumbs
1½ tsp salt
½ tsp freshly ground black pepper

2 tbsp chopped fresh dill
½ tsp ground cinnamon
¼ tsp ground cloves
1 garlic clove, crushed
1 tsp finely grated
  fresh ginger

1 tsp Worcestershire
  sauce or lemon juice
1 egg, beaten
dry breadcrumbs, for coating
oil or ghee, for deep-frying

METHOD

Heat the butter in a small frying pan over a low heat. Add the onion and cook until it is soft. Cool slightly and place in a bowl along with the minced beef, breadcrumbs, salt, pepper, dill, cinnamon, cloves, garlic, ginger and Worcestershire sauce. Use your hands to combine thoroughly.

Shape the mince mixture into small balls, diameter 2.5 cm. Put the egg in a bowl and the dry breadcrumbs in a shallow dish. Dip each meatball first into the egg and then roll in the dry breadcrumbs to coat, shaking off any excess.

Heat the oil in a deep-fryer or large heavy-based frying pan and deep-fry the balls until golden-brown. Drain on paper towel before serving as an accompaniment.

VAMBOTU PAHI
EGGPLANT PICKLE

PREP TIME: 1 HOUR | COOK TIME: 35 MINS | SKILL LEVEL: 1 (EASY)

INGREDIENTS

2 tsp salt, plus extra
  to taste

2 tsp turmeric

2 large eggplants, cut
  into slices 1 cm thick

oil for frying

1 tbsp black mustard seeds

125 ml (½ cup) vinegar

1 onion, finely chopped

4 garlic cloves, sliced

1 tbsp finely chopped
  fresh ginger

1 tbsp ground coriander

2 tsp ground cumin

1 tsp ground fennel

125 g (½ cup)
  tamarind pulp

3 fresh green chillies,
  de-seeded and sliced

8 cm stick cinnamon

1 tsp chilli powder
  (optional)

2 tsp sugar

METHOD

Rub the salt and turmeric over the eggplant slices and drain in a colander for at least 1 hour. Dry with paper towel.

Heat oil to a depth of about 2.5 cm in a large, heavy-based frying pan. Add the eggplant and cook until brown on both sides. Remove to a plate, reserving 125 ml (½ cup) of oil in the pan.

Put the mustard seeds and vinegar into a food processor and process to a pulp. Add the onion, garlic and ginger, and process to a smooth paste. Set aside.

Dry-fry the coriander, cumin and fennel in a small frying pan over a low heat, shaking the pan or stirring, until toasted.

Soak the tamarind pulp in 185 ml (¾ cup) of hot water for 10 minutes. Squeeze to dissolve the pulp in the water, then strain, discarding the seeds and fibre.

Heat the reserved oil and cook the mustard seed mixture for 5 minutes. Add the toasted spices, fresh chilli, cinnamon, tamarind liquid and chilli powder (if using). Add the eggplant and any oil, cover, and simmer for 15 minutes. Remove from the heat, stir in the sugar and add salt to taste.

Cool and store in sterilised airtight jars.

TIPS

The eggplant pickle will keep for many months. To avoid spoiling, always use a clean dry spoon.

SEENI SAMBOLA
CHILLI SAMBOL

MAKES: 2 CUPS | PREP TIME: 10 MINS | COOK TIME: 20 MINS | SKILL LEVEL: 1 (EASY)

INGREDIENTS

125 ml (½ cup) oil

4 onions, thinly sliced

2 tsp chilli powder, or to taste

170 g canned 'prawns in spices' (available in Asian grocery stores)

2 tbsp vinegar

1 tsp sugar

METHOD

Heat the oil in a large frying pan over a low heat. Add the onion and cook until soft. It is important to cook the onion slowly – the liquid in the onion must evaporate if the sambol is to keep well.

When the onion is golden-brown, add the chilli powder, 'prawns in spices' and vinegar. Stir thoroughly, cover, and simmer for 10 minutes. Uncover the pan and continue simmering, stirring occasionally, until the liquid evaporates and the oil starts to separate.

Season with salt to taste. Remove from the heat, stir in the sugar and allow to cool. Spoon into a sterilised airtight jar; keeps for up to one month. Use in small quantities.

PRAWN BLACAN

SERVINGS: 18–20 | PREP TIME: 15 MINS | SKILL LEVEL: 1 (EASY)

INGREDIENTS

250 g (1 cup) dried prawn powder

45 g (½ cup) desiccated coconut

2 tsp chilli powder, or to taste

2 onions, chopped

5 cloves garlic, sliced

1 tbsp finely chopped fresh ginger

170 ml (⅔ cup) lemon juice

1 tsp salt, or to taste

METHOD

Heat the prawn powder in a dry frying pan over a low heat for a few minutes, stirring. Remove to a plate. Put the coconut in the same pan and heat, stirring, until a rich chestnut-brown colour. Remove to a plate.

Put the remaining ingredients into a food processor and blend until smooth. Add the prawn powder and coconut and process to combine, adding a little water to bind the ingredients if needed. Place on a plate and shape into a round, flat cake. Serve with rice and curries.

FLOWERPOT.
TAS

DAVID MOYLE
FRANKLIN

WOOD-GRILLED CALAMARI SALAD

FOR ME, COOKING IS NOT SO MUCH TECHNICAL
AS IT IS OBSERVATIONAL. THAT'S HOW I LIKE
TO COOK, TO BE AS CONNECTED AS I CAN.
THERE IS SOMETHING ABOUT EATING FOOD OUTSIDE
IN THE ENVIRONMENT IT HAS BEEN COOKED THAT
MAKES YOU APPRECIATE IT MUCH MORE.

— DAVE.

WOOD-GRILLED CALAMARI SALAD

SERVINGS: 4 AS AN ENTRÉE | PREP TIME: 45 MINS | SKILL LEVEL: 2 (MODERATE)

INGREDIENTS

4 cloves garlic
100 ml light olive oil
1 kg Southern calamari
  (legs, wings and hoods)
1 Lebanese cucumber
1 shallot
2 cups fennel fronds
juice of ½ lemon
50 g fresh horseradish
1 tsp dried fennel pollen
  (see tip)

METHOD

Set up a wood-fired grill well ahead of time – the best results are from a fire that is mostly coals, so that the grilling is achieved by dry heat on the calamari, not flames or contact heat from the wire of the grill cage.

Peel the garlic and crush in a mortar and pestle to a consistent size – each piece should be approximately 1 mm x 1 mm but of varying shape. Place in a heavy-based pot over a medium-high heat, together with the oil. Bring up to frying temperature and keep agitating until the garlic goes a golden-brown. Remove from the heat and let it cool. The colour of the garlic is of the utmost importance: too light and the garlic is astringent; too much colour and the garlic is bitter.

Gut, peel and clean the calamari. Avoid using fresh water, as it taints the flesh and starts decomposition; wiping with paper towel is very effective. Open the hoods of the calamari and place in a grill cage; place the legs and wings in another cage, as these cuts require more cooking. Grill briefly on both sides, trying to avoid flames licking the squid or placing it too close to the heat source. The cooking time depends on the size of the calamari, the heat of the fire and how close the calamari is to the heat, and can take anywhere from 1–6 minutes for both sides. When ready, the calamari should be mostly translucent.

Peel and finely shred the cucumber, season lightly with salt and place in the bottom of a mixing bowl. Peel and shred the shallot even more finely and pick the fennel fronds, placing both over the cucumber. Very finely shred the calamari and place to the side of the cucumber, shallot and fennel.

Dress the calamari with the garlic-flavoured oil and the lemon juice. Season lightly, remembering (fondly) the salt that is already on the cucumber. Toss the calamari, then gently involve the fennel and cucumber mixture. Place in a serving bowl and grate horseradish over the top. Sprinkle with fennel pollen.

TIP

Dried fennel pollen can be bought in specialist stores, though it's very expensive. If you grow fennel, it's easy to make your own. Pick flower heads that are open and yellow (check there are no bugs on them), place in a paper bag and leave to dry in the sun for a few days. Shake the stems to release the pollen into the bag, then shake gently through a fine sieve to remove stems and other unwanted parts.

MERLE PARRISH

PEACH BLOSSOM CAKE
ANZAC BISCUITS
PAVLOVA

Half the fun of life is to share recipes with someone else, and that was the reason why I wrote my cookbooks. A lot of the recipes I share are ones that I've had through my family and ones that I've had for many years. And why not share them if someone wants to know what they are? — Merle

NANA'S PLACE
~ WHERE ALL HER LITTLE CUPCAKES GET SPRINKLED WITH LOVE ~

CUDAL, NSW

PEACH BLOSSOM CAKE

SERVINGS: 8 | PREP TIME: 30 MINS | COOK TIME: 1 HOUR 10 MINS | SKILL LEVEL: 2 (MODERATE)

INGREDIENTS

190 g butter at room temperature, chopped
1¼ cups white sugar
¾ cup milk
1 tsp vanilla essence
1½ cups plain flour
¾ cup cornflour
1½ tsp baking powder
pinch of salt
6 egg whites
1–2 drops rose-pink food colouring

Icing
1½ cups icing sugar
10 g butter
2 tbsp boiling water
few drops of rose-pink food colouring

METHOD

Pre-heat the oven to low (150°C). Grease a 20 cm round, deep cake tin. Line the base of the tin with baking paper.

Cream the butter and sugar in the small bowl of an electric mixer until white and fluffy. Gradually add half the milk to help dissolve the sugar, and beat well. Beat in the vanilla. Transfer to a larger bowl.

Sift the flour, cornflour, baking powder and salt together three times. Fold into the butter mixture, then add the remaining milk (don't worry if it appears curdled at this stage).

In another bowl, use clean beaters to beat the egg whites to stiff peaks. Fold half the egg whites into the cake batter, then fold in the remaining egg whites.

Transfer 1 cup of the mixture to a smaller bowl, and stir in the drops of food colouring. Take about ¾ cup of the white mixture, and spread over the base of the tin. Take half the pink batter, and spoon it in a ring about 1 cm in from the edge of the tin – it should be about 1–1½ cm wide.

Very carefully spread half the remaining white batter over, taking care not to disturb the pink ring. Spoon the remaining pink batter into the centre of the tin, making a round of about 8 cm. Spoon the rest of the white batter over the whole top, again taking care not to disturb the pink round.

Bake for about 1 hour 10 minutes, until the cake is springy to a gentle touch in the centre and comes away from the sides of the tin. It may appear slightly cracked in the centre, but should settle flat on cooling. (If not, gently press the top flat with your fingertips.) Turn out onto a clean tea towel lined with a sheet of baking paper. Leave to cool.

To make the icing, combine the ingredients until smooth. Spread over the top of the cooled cake, and leave to set.

ANZAC BISCUITS

MAKES: 45 | PREP TIME: 20 MINS | COOK TIME: 6 MINS PER BATCH | SKILL LEVEL: 1 (EASY)

INGREDIENTS

1 cup plain flour
2 tsp ground ginger
1½ cups rolled oats
1 cup desiccated coconut
1 cup white sugar
1 tbsp golden syrup
2 tbsp boiling water
1 tsp bicarbonate of soda
160 g butter, melted

METHOD

Pre-heat the oven to moderate (170°C) and grease two large baking trays.

Sift the flour and ground ginger into a mixing bowl, and add the oats, coconut and sugar. Make a well in the centre.

Stir the golden syrup, boiling water and bicarbonate in a small bowl until combined. Add to the dry ingredients, along with the melted butter. Mix well.

Take heaped teaspoons of the mixture and roll into balls. Place onto the trays and flatten gently. Leave 2–2½ cm between each ball. Bake for 6–7 minutes, until lightly golden. You will probably need to bake in several batches.

Cool on the trays for 10 minutes once out of the oven, until they firm up slightly, then lift onto wire racks to cool completely.

PAVLOVA

INGREDIENTS

6 egg whites
1½ cups caster sugar
1½ tsp white vinegar
1 tbsp cornflour
whipped cream, to serve
1–2 passionfruit, to serve
berries, to serve

METHOD

Pre-heat the oven to very low (120°C). Grease a baking tray and line it with a sheet of baking paper. Draw a 22 cm circle on the back of the baking paper.

Use an electric mixer to beat the egg whites until stiff peaks form. Add sugar, 1 tablespoon at a time, beating between each addition until the sugar has dissolved. Keep adding and beating until the mixture is thick, white and glossy. Beat in the vinegar and cornflour.

Use a large spoon to transfer the mixture to the baking tray, then shape into a 22 cm round. Bake for 1½ hours, then turn off the oven, prop the door open slightly and leave to cool completely.

When cool, top with whipped cream, berries and passionfruit.

RODNEY DUNN
THE AGRARIAN KITCHEN

APPLE & BERRY CRUMBLE
WITH VANILLA CUSTARD

Everything I do revolves around the seasons. I love apples, grew up with apple crumble, which was what Mum used to make and is probably my all-time favourite. If I had a birthday, the old apple crumble would be my choice. So it was something that sort of naturally came to mind when I was thinking of something that is dear to me and is very Australian.

Rodney

APPLE & BERRY CRUMBLE WITH VANILLA CUSTARD

SERVINGS: 6 | PREP TIME: 40 MINS | COOK TIME: 35–40 MINS | SKILL LEVEL: 1 (EASY)

INGREDIENTS

1.4 kg apples

275 g sugar

1 vanilla bean,
  split lengthways

1½ cups raspberries

Vanilla custard

500 ml milk

400 ml cream

1 vanilla bean,
  split lengthways

240 g egg yolk
  (from about 10 eggs)

200 g caster sugar

Crumble mixture

150 g plain flour

120 g cold butter,
  finely chopped

90 g raw sugar

pinch of salt

50 g flaked almonds

METHOD

Peel and core apples and cut into 2 cm pieces. Place in a large saucepan with sugar and vanilla, cover and cook over a medium heat, stirring occasionally, until apples are soft and have broken apart; about 15–20 minutes. Remove from heat, add raspberries and carefully fold through. Remove vanilla bean and discard.

For vanilla custard: combine milk, cream and vanilla bean in a large saucepan and bring to the boil over a medium-high heat. Place egg yolks and sugar in a bowl, whisk until just combined, then gradually pour hot milk mixture into the bowl and whisk to combine. Return mixture to the same saucepan and stir over a low heat until mixture reaches 83°C; it will thicken enough to coat the back of a wooden spoon. Do not boil. Remove vanilla bean, scrape out seeds and stir seeds through custard.

For crumble mixture: place flour, butter, sugar and salt in a bowl and use your fingertips to rub the ingredients together, then mix almonds through.

Pre-heat oven to 200°C. Spoon apple and raspberry mixture into six ovenproof ramekins or one large ovenproof dish. Scatter with crumble mixture and place in the oven. Cook until the crumble is golden-brown and the mixture is beginning to bubble up the sides; 35–40 minutes.

Serve with vanilla custard.

NEIL PERRY AM

SPICY PRAWN TORTILLAS

Being a restaurateur means I'm not always home for dinner with the family, so I love it when my girls come visit me after school & have an early dinner together. This recipe is how we like to eat at home : very relaxed, informal & hands-on.

Neil

SYDNEY, NSW

SPICY PRAWN TORTILLAS

SERVINGS: 4 | PREP TIME: 20 MINS PLUS MARINATING | SKILL LEVEL: 1 (EASY)

INGREDIENTS

Prawns
600 g green king prawns
3 cloves garlic, crushed
1 large Spanish onion, finely diced
1 tsp cumin seeds
1 tsp coriander seeds
2 tsp salsa macha
1 tsp sea salt
100 ml extra virgin olive oil
juice of 2 limes

Salsa
5 Roma tomatoes
4 chipotles in adobo (see tip below)
sea salt to taste

Salad
2 cups shaved cabbage
2 cucumbers peeled, halved, seeded
   and cut into ½ cm semi-circles
½ a bunch of coriander leaves,
   washed and chopped

To serve
tortillas, enough to serve 4 people

METHOD

Peel and de-vein the prawns. In a bowl, mix the prawns with all the ingredients except the lime juice and leave to marinate for an hour.

Finely dice the tomatoes and finely mince the chipotles. Mix the salsa ingredients together with a sprinkle of sea salt and place in a small serving bowl.

Mix all the salad ingredients and place in a serving bowl.

To finish, heat a grill pan or pan to hot. Add the prawns and marinade, cook quickly on one side and toss to cook on the other. Don't overcook – it will happen quickly. Place the prawns in a serving bowl and squeeze the lime juice over. Heat the tortillas in a microwave.

Place all the dishes in the middle of the table, take a tortilla and spoon a bit of each dish on, roll and enjoy.

TIP

Salsa macha is a traditional chilli salsa from the Oaxacan and Veracruz regions in Mexico, made with extra virgin olive oil. It is available in specialty food stores, as are the chipotles in adobo, a spicy Mexican sauce (adobo) of smoke-dried jalapeños (chipotle).

ABLA AMAD AM
ABLA'S LEBANESE RESTAURANT

DJAJ A RIZ
BAKLAWA

I love people. Like last night, the restaurant was full and, believe me, I checked every table to see if people enjoyed their meals. Before I could say anything, they said, "It's beautiful, Abla!" It makes me feel like I haven't even done an hour's work!

Abla

TOORAK, VIC

DJAJ A RIZ
CHICKEN & RICE

SERVINGS: 6–8 | PREP TIME: 1 HOUR | SKILL LEVEL: 1 (EASY)

INGREDIENTS

500–600 g whole
chicken breasts on
the bone, skin on

1 stick cinnamon

2½ tsp salt

600 g coarsely
minced lean lamb

20 g butter

½ tsp freshly ground
black pepper

½ tsp allspice

½ tsp ground cinnamon,
plus extra to garnish

1½ cups (300 g)
long-grain rice,
washed and drained

olive oil, for cooking

½ cup (80 g) pine nuts

½ cup (40 g) flaked
or slivered almonds

(GF)

METHOD

Place the chicken breasts in a large saucepan and cover with water. Add cinnamon and 1 tsp of the salt and bring to the boil, then reduce the heat to low and simmer, covered, for 20–30 minutes or until tender and cooked through. Drain, reserving the stock. Remove the skin and tear the meat from the bone (the chicken slivers can be any size). Set aside.

Cook the minced lamb in a saucepan in its own juices over a medium heat for about 10 minutes, mashing with a wooden spoon to separate any lumps, and stirring regularly to avoid it sticking. Stir in the butter, pepper, spices and remaining salt. Cover and cook for 20 minutes or until well done, stirring regularly to prevent lumps forming. Add the rice and 2½ cups (625 ml) of the reserved chicken stock, then cover and cook for a further 20 minutes.

Heat a little olive oil in a frying pan and cook the pine nuts and almonds over a medium heat for 3–4 minutes or until golden, stirring constantly to prevent burning. Remove the nuts with a slotted spoon and drain on paper towel.

To assemble, spread the pine nuts and almonds over the base of a 25 cm round cake tin with a hollow centre. Pack the shredded chicken around the sides of the mould. Fill with the lamb and rice mixture, pressing down firmly and ensuring that the chicken remains in place.

To serve, put a serving plate face down over the mould and invert the chicken and rice onto it. Gently remove the mould and sprinkle a little extra cinnamon over the top.

Another way to serve this is to put the lamb and rice mixture on a serving dish and cover it with the chicken. Top with the pine nuts and slivered almonds, and finish with a dusting of ground cinnamon.

BAKLAWA
A CLASSIC LEBANESE SWEET

MAKES: ABOUT 25 | PREP TIME: 45 MINS | COOK TIME: 45 MINS | SKILL LEVEL: 2 (MODERATE)

INGREDIENTS

1 x 375 g packet
filo pastry

250 g unsalted
butter, melted

2 cups (260 g) finely
ground cashews

½ quantity thick sugar
syrup (see below), hot

¼ cup (30 g) coarsely
ground pistachio nuts
(optional)

Thick sugar syrup (attir)

800 g white sugar

1 tbsp lemon juice

2½ cups (625 ml) water

1 tbsp rose-water

METHOD

To make the syrup, bring the sugar, lemon juice and water to the boil over a medium heat. Cover and boil for 20 minutes, until the sugar has completely dissolved and the syrup is thick. Stir in the rose-water and remove from the heat. Depending on the occasion, use while still hot or allow to cool and store in an airtight container in the fridge for up to two weeks.

Pre-heat the oven to 220°C. Cut the filo pastry sheets to the size of your baking tin: a good size is 25 cm x 35 cm. Brush the baking tin liberally with melted butter. Layer half the filo pastry sheets into the tin, brushing every second sheet with butter. Spread the cashews evenly over the pastry. Cover with the remaining filo, brushing every second sheet with butter. Do not butter the top layer yet.

With a sharp knife, make parallel cuts on the diagonal, about 3½ cm apart, through to the base of the tin. Then cut on the diagonal the other way, to create diamond shapes. Brush the remaining butter on top.

Bake for 10 minutes, then reduce the temperature to 180°C and bake for another 35 minutes or until golden. Remove from the oven. Pour the hot syrup over the hot pastry. Sprinkle with pistachio nuts (if using) and leave to cool.

NIKKI & DOUG GOVAN
STAR OF GREECE

SALT & PEPPER SQUID WITH LEMON & GARLIC MAYO
ALE-BATTERED KING GEORGE WHITING
WITH HAND-CUT CHIPS

Sunset is unbeatable.
But even in the middle of winter,
looking out in to the storms & waves,
it's always fantastic to look out
over the water.
We like to sit on the deck having
a glass of wine and watching the
sun sink in to the ocean.
Whether we're with family or just
the two of us, it's peaceful and
a very nice place to be.

Nikki & Doug

PORT WILLUNGA,
SA

SALT & PEPPER SQUID
WITH LEMON & GARLIC MAYO

SERVINGS: *5* | PREP TIME: *20 MINS* | SKILL LEVEL: *2 (MODERATE)*

INGREDIENTS

Lemon and garlic mayo
2 whole eggs
2 egg yolks
1 tsp Dijon mustard
½ tsp minced garlic
400 ml olive oil
juice of 1 lemon

oil for deep-frying
2 whole fresh squid
1 bottle soda water
250 g coarse rice flour

METHOD

Make the lemon and garlic mayo by blending eggs, yolks, mustard and garlic in an electric mixer until creamy and light. Slowly and steadily beat in olive oil. Once combined, mix in lemon juice and set aside.

Heat oil in a deep-fryer to 180°C.

Clean the squid by cutting the tentacles off the body; reserve the tentacles. Pull the head, guts and feather out of the squid tube in one motion, and discard. Clean the squid tube by scraping the membrane away from the flesh, keeping the wings on the body. Slice the tube into rings about 1 cm thick and add to the tentacles.

Wash squid with soda water, then drain in a colander. Once drained, toss squid in rice flour, shake off extra flour and deep-fry for about 30–40 seconds. Toss squid with sea salt and freshly ground black pepper to taste, and serve with the lemon and garlic mayo.

ALE-BATTERED KING GEORGE WHITING
WITH HAND-CUT CHIPS

SERVINGS: *4* | PREP TIME: *5 MINS* | COOK TIME: *30 MINS PLUS CHILLING* | SKILL LEVEL: *1 (EASY)*

INGREDIENTS

Hand-cut chips
oil for deep-frying
8 medium Désirée
  potatoes

Fish
oil for deep-frying
8 fillets King George
  whiting (or any
  other delicate
  white-fleshed fish)
225 g self-raising flour
1 bottle sparkling ale
  (we use Coopers)
plain flour to coat

METHOD

Heat oil to 180°C in a deep-fryer.

Slice potatoes lengthways into eighths. Plunge them, all at once, into the hot oil in the deep-fryer and immediately turn the temperature down to 120°C. Cook for 10–15 minutes or until chips are cooked but still firm. Spread out on a large tray and cool in the fridge. Turn deep-fryer back up to 180°C.

Cut the fins off and pin-bones out from the whiting fillets.

To make the batter, slowly whisk the flour into the ale, whisking until you have a smooth batter.

When ready to cook, toss the fillets a few at a time in enough plain flour to coat. Dip the fillets into the batter and carefully lower them into the hot oil. The fish will float and needs to be turned over once the bottom side is a nice light golden colour (this should take about 1 minute). Continue to fry until evenly coloured on that side, then remove fish and drain on a paper towel.

Fry chilled chips at 180°C until golden and crisp. Season with salt and serve with the fish.

HOBART,
TAS

EMMA & JAY PATEY
PIGEON WHOLE BAKERS

EASY-BAKE SOURDOUGH
LAMINGTONS

Going to the bakery on a weekend
morning is a memory of growing up.
Often there would be lamingtons in
the cabinet and so they have an
association with a childhood treat.
Keep the jam and cream for scones;
it's all about a good sponge and
great coconut and chocolate.

Jay + Emma.

EASY-BAKE SOURDOUGH

SERVINGS: 1 LOAF | PREP TIME: 1–2 DAYS | COOK TIME: 35 MINS | SKILL LEVEL: 2 (MODERATE)

INGREDIENTS

500 g whole spelt flour

380 g water,
at room temperature

110 g leaven (60 g wheat
flour, 50 g water; we
use organic stoneground
white wheat flour)

9 g sea salt

METHOD

First, let the flour hydrate (autolyse) for an hour: add spelt flour and water to a medium-sized bowl, mix by hand until just combined and then let it rest. *To prepare leaven:* Day 1: mix 60 g of flour and 50 g water and leave in a warm place in the kitchen, covered; Day 2: repeat the same step adding to the original amount; Day 3: remove one third of the mixture then repeat step 1. If you want to keep a starter dough, you can reserve what you have removed to feed the starter (see below); Day 4: it will be ready to use. Once your starter is at this point it can be stored in the fridge and fed once a week to maintain its health. The day before you require it, remove it from the fridge and feed and leave it at room temperature.

The final mix requires the addition of the leaven and salt, mixing in by hand and then continuing to fold and turn the dough for a few minutes. Cover and allow to rest again, in a warm spot in your kitchen. This is what I call the bulk ferment stage: over the next 2 hours, give the dough another two series of gentle folds and turns, as if you are folding up a large blanket. At this point the dough should have increased in volume.

Now, gently form the dough into a nice tight ball, with the top surface being nice and smooth, and place it in a floured banneton (bread-proving) basket, seam side to the sky. At this stage either cover and place in the fridge overnight (a minimum of 8 hours and a maximum of 14 hours; once removed from the fridge allow to rest at room temperature for 1 hour), or cover and leave in a warm spot for a further 3–4 hours.

Baking requires the oven to be at 250°C. Pre-heat a cast-iron Dutch oven (or casserole). Flour the warmed Dutch oven, then gently remove the dough from the banneton and place it in the Dutch oven. Cover with the lid and place in the oven to bake. After 20 minutes, remove the lid and bake for another 10–15 minutes. Turn out onto a rack to cool.

LAMINGTONS

MAKES: 20 | PREP TIME: 30 MINS PLUS COOLING | COOK TIME: 20 MINS | SKILL LEVEL: 2 (MODERATE)

INGREDIENTS

8 eggs (if possible
home-grown)

240 g caster sugar

240 g plain flour, sifted

20 g butter, melted

1 tsp vanilla extract

400 g good-quality dark
chocolate chips
(65–70%; we use
Callebaut Callets)

200 g pure cream

500 g shredded coconut

METHOD

When preparing the sponge, it's essential to have the oven pre-heated to 190°C, a 25 cm x 25 cm baking tin already greased and lined with baking paper, the butter melted and all ingredients measured and ready to hand.

In the bowl of a stand mixer, whisk by hand, over a simmering water bath, eggs and caster sugar until dissolved and at 38–40°C. Return bowl to stand mixer with whisk attachment and whisk for around 8 minutes on medium to high speed, until tripled in volume.

Remove the bowl from the stand mixer. Gently add a small amount of flour at intervals, incorporating with a silicone spatula and adding melted butter and vanilla just before the last addition of flour. Do not overwork the batter! Place in prepared tin and bake straightaway for about 20 minutes until the surface is light brown. Remove from oven and cool on a wire rack before cutting into 20 pieces.

When the sponge is portioned, melt chocolate over a water bath in a large bowl, then incorporate cream. Spread coconut out on a flat tray. Dip sponge into chocolate on all sides, then onto the tray of coconut, then onto a wire rack to set.

Lamingtons will keep for up to three days in an airtight container – good luck keeping them that long!

CHRISTIANA MONOSTORI
YATI'S LAKSA AND SHAVED
ICE AT PARAP VILLAGE MARKETS

YATI'S CHICKEN LAKSA

AT THE MARKET WE SOCIALISE, MEET PEOPLE AND IT'S LIKE A FAMILY. MY CUSTOMERS TELL ME WHEN THEY GO ON HOLIDAYS, AND WHEN THEY COME BACK THEY SAY "OH... WE MISSED YOUR LAKSA!".

CHRISTIANA.

YATI'S CHICKEN LAKSA

SERVINGS: 2 | PREP TIME: 20–25 MINS | SKILL LEVEL: 1 (EASY)

INGREDIENTS

1 chicken breast
(or 2 thigh fillets if
you prefer dark meat)

4 cups home-made chicken
stock (or a good-quality
commercial liquid stock)

1 large white onion,
peeled and quartered

1 stalk fresh lemongrass,
coarsely chopped

vegetable oil for frying

1 x 185 g jar Malaysian
laksa paste

1 x 400 ml can
coconut milk

1 packet of your favourite
fresh noodles (egg
noodles, flat rice noodles,
Hokkien noodles or rice
vermicelli are great)

Garnish options

1 long red chilli,
finely sliced

dried chilli flakes
(if you like it hot)

2–3 tbsp fried onions
(from any Asian grocer)

handful of fresh
coriander leaves

METHOD

In a small pot on medium to high heat, pour the chicken stock and add the chicken breast (or thighs). Bring the meat to the boil and then immediately turn the heat down and allow the chicken to simmer for 15–20 minutes or until tender. Remove the cooked meat from the stock and once cool enough to handle, shred the chicken into pieces. Reserve the stock for the laksa.

In a food processor, blend together the onion and lemongrass until a coarse paste is achieved. To a heavy-based pot on a medium heat, add 1 tablespoon of vegetable oil and, once hot, fry off the onion and lemongrass paste for 2–3 minutes until the rawness of the onion has been cooked out.

Add the ready-made laksa paste and stir-fry this combined mixture for a further 3–4 minutes until fragrant. Add two cups of the chicken stock and the can of coconut milk, bring the mixture to the boil, then immediately reduce to low heat until ready to serve. Season to taste.

To serve, place the fresh noodles in the simmering laksa and cook until tender. Scoop out the noodles and place one serve in each bowl. Place some of the shredded chicken on top of the noodles and gently ladle the laksa over the top of the chicken and noodles. Top the bowl with your choice of garnish ingredients.

ANDREW PUGLISI
KINKAWOOKA SHELLFISH

BARBECUED PRAWNS
WITH HERBED BUTTER
STEAMED POT OF MUSSELS

My Nonno left Lipari in Italy when he was nineteen years old. He left with the clothes on his back and a suitcase, and in that suitcase was a fishing longline. When he arrived in Australia, he went out on Sydney Harbour in a tiny fishing boat to catch fish, and with that longline he was able to earn enough money to bring our whole family to Australia — and here we are today, five generations of fishermen later.

Pugs.

PORT LINCOLN, SA

BARBECUED PRAWNS WITH HERBED BUTTER

SERVINGS: 4 | PREP TIME: 10 MINS | COOK TIME: 3 MINS | SKILL LEVEL: 1 (EASY)

INGREDIENTS

1 kg jumbo (U/6 or U/8) Spencer Gulf king prawns

150 g good-quality cultured butter, softened

1 clove garlic, crushed

1 tsp chopped fresh oregano

1 tbsp chopped fresh flat-leaf parsley

METHOD

Thaw your prawns (you can also use fresh prawns if you don't have Spencer Gulf king prawns) and, using a sharp knife, cut through the shell down the back of each prawn, but not all the way through. This will allow you to de-vein the prawn and create a cavity for your herbed butter.

Combine the butter, garlic and herbs in a mixing bowl and spoon a generous amount of the mixture into the cavity of each prawn.

Heat your barbecue flat-plate until very hot and barbecue the prawns for 1–1½ minutes on each side. The prawns will continue to cook after they are removed from the heat, so don't worry about undercooking them.

Serve with a green salad and some crusty bread to mop up all those buttery juices.

STEAMED POT OF MUSSELS

SERVINGS: 2 | PREP TIME: 10 MINS | COOK TIME: 10 MINS | SKILL LEVEL: 1 (EASY)

INGREDIENTS

1 kg cleaned, fresh mussels

150 ml good-quality olive oil

2 cloves garlic, chopped

handful Italian parsley, chopped

METHOD

Place your largest pot, wok or frying pan on a high heat, add the mussels and pop on the lid. Stir 2–3 times over the next 4–5 minutes, and when the mussels have opened and the meat has separated from the outside edge of the shell, they are cooked. Empty the mussels into the sink or a bowl (you can reserve the mussel stock to use later on for a fantastic risotto or fish stew).

Meanwhile, heat the olive oil in a large wok or frying pan, add the garlic and gently fry for 1 minute. Add the mussels and parsley and toss through until all of the mussels are covered in the oil and are heated through.

Serve straight from the wok or frying pan in the middle of the dinner table, with some crusty bread for dipping into that lovely sauce.

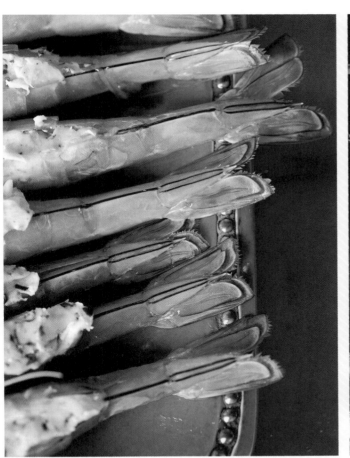

MATT & MARCELA O'DONOHUE VALENCIA
MARCELITA'S EMPANADAS

EMPANADAS DE RES
AJÍ PIQUE
FRIJOLES PAISAS

The first time Marcela made empanadas for me was in the kitchen of her tiny apartment. She was rolling out balls of dough, filling them, and dropping them into a small pot bubbling with oil. I tried one and was stunned — "These are amazing! How have I gone my whole life without trying them!?" From then on I was hooked, on Marcela, and on empanadas.

Matt O'Donohue

SUBIACO, WA

EMPANADAS DE RES
COLOMBIAN BEEF EMPANADAS

MAKES: APPROX. 40 | PREP TIME: 1½ – 2 HOURS | SKILL LEVEL: 2 (MODERATE)

INGREDIENTS

Dough

500 g maize flour
(yellow harina P.A.N.)

2 tbsp cumin seeds

2 tbsp table salt

2 tsp triguisar
(Colombian spice mixture,
available from Latin
American stores)

1 tsp bicarbonate of soda

1–2 litres warm water

Filling

250 g waxy potatoes
(e.g. Royal Blue),
unpeeled and
roughly chopped

500 g beef skirt,
fat removed and
cut into strips

2 cups chopped tomato
(seeds and all)

2 cups finely chopped
spring onion

¼ cup olive oil

1 tbsp cumin seeds

½ cup chopped coriander

high-smoke-point oil
(cottonseed, canola),
for deep-frying

METHOD

Dough: place the flour into a large bowl and mix all the other dry ingredients into it. Gradually add the warm water and knead the mixture in the bowl until it starts to come together and all the dry flour is absorbed. When the mixture has formed a soft, pliable dough that can be rolled into a ball and squashed flat, it's ready.

Filling: in a large pot of salted water, boil the potatoes for about 20 minutes, or until they are just tender enough to mash. Squash them roughly and set aside to cool down.

Season the beef skirt with salt and place it in a pot or pressure cooker, with just enough water to cover. Cook until the beef is tender and falling apart (approximately 45 minutes in a pot, 20 minutes in a pressure cooker).

Fry the tomato and spring onion together with a good splash of olive oil, add the cumin seeds and salt and pepper to taste, and cook until the tomato and onion break down into a thick sauce.

Shred the cooked beef by hand or with two forks, and work it together with the potato and tomato mixture. Once it has come together, add the coriander and finally season the whole mixture with salt and pepper to taste.

To finish: take a golf-ball-sized ball of dough and place it between two sheets of plastic film or baking paper. Squash the ball into a flat disc – as thin as possible without it breaking. Take a tablespoon of the filling and place it in the centre of the dough; then, holding the bottom sheet of plastic wrap or paper, fold one side of the dough over the top of the filling. Press down lightly to form a seal, and use a cookie cutter or a glass to fully seal the empanada. Place it on a flat surface, ready to be fried.

Heat a deep-fryer or a deep pot filled with oil to 180°C, and fry the empanadas until the shell is hard and crispy and they are a deep golden colour (3–5 minutes).

Eat immediately with some Colombian Chilli Salsa (Ají Pique) or guacamole.

AJÍ PIQUE
COLOMBIAN CHILLI SALSA

MAKES: APPROX. 1 LITRE | PREP TIME: 20 MINS | SKILL LEVEL: 1 (EASY)

INGREDIENTS

500 g long red chillies

100 ml white vinegar

500 ml cold water

2 tbsp salt

100 g powdered or
grated Colombian
panela (or raw sugar)

2 cups finely chopped
spring onion

2 cups finely chopped
coriander

METHOD

Trim the ends off the chillies and, leaving them whole (seeds and all), place them in a blender and blend until they form a thick pulp.

Pour the chilli pulp into a large bowl, and slowly add the vinegar, water, salt and panela, while stirring. Then add the spring onion and coriander and mix through well.

It's important to taste as you go as the heat level of the chillies can vary a lot. You may need to add more water or panela to counterbalance the heat.

Pour the mixture into containers and store in the fridge. It can be used immediately, but the flavour will develop after some time resting. This salsa will keep in the fridge for up to a month (if it lasts that long!).

FRIJOLES PAISAS
COLOMBIAN BEAN STEW

SERVINGS: 4–6 | PREP TIME: 10 MINS PLUS SOAKING
COOK TIME: 1¼ HOURS | SKILL LEVEL: 1 (EASY)

INGREDIENTS

500 g pork belly,
  cut into thick strips
1 cup dried red kidney beans
2 cups dried borlotti beans
1 litre vegetable stock
2 brown onions, finely diced
2 cloves garlic, finely chopped
½ cup finely chopped coriander roots
  (just the roots)
4 carrots, peeled

1 tbsp salt
4 medium tomatoes, finely diced
½ cup finely chopped spring onion
½ tbsp cumin seeds
olive oil for cooking

To garnish
¼ cup coriander leaves
1 avocado
wedges of lime

METHOD

Pre-heat the oven to 180°C. Cover the beans in cold (unsalted) water and soak for 2 hours.

Season the pork belly well with salt. Place in the oven and roast for 1 hour, turning occasionally to make sure it cooks evenly on all sides. For the last 5 minutes, increase the heat and change the oven to grill, making sure the pork belly is skin-side up to crisp the top and create crackle. Cut the pork into thick chunks, to add to the beans later.

Drain the beans and place in a large pot on the stove along with the stock, and add the onion, garlic, coriander roots, whole carrots and salt. Add extra water to cover the ingredients if necessary. Cook on a medium heat for approximately 45 minutes, occasionally checking the beans for softness.

When the carrots are cooked through, remove them from the pot and place them in a blender with 1 cup of the cooking liquid. Blend to make a purée, and add the puréed carrots back to the pot. Continue cooking the beans until they are slightly al dente, and the stock has reduced and thickened.

In a frying pan, fry the tomato, spring onion and cumin seeds together with a little olive oil until they break down into a rich salsa. This is called 'guiso' and is mixed through the beans at the end to give extra flavour.

When the beans are ready, mix in the guiso and pork belly chunks and warm for 5 minutes.

Garnish beans with coriander leaves, slices of avocado and wedges of freshly cut lime, and serve alongside white rice.

JILL DUPLEIX

SLASHED ROAST LEG OF LAMB
CRASH-HOT POTATOES

I grew up on a sheep farm in Victoria, and these are two of my all-time favourite recipes — they're practical, sturdy and designed to share.

The roast leg of lamb is symbolic for so many Australians — it's our comfort food. The beautiful sweet meat takes on all the flavours and influences of the world — as do the crash-hot potatoes.

As do Australians, come to think of it.

Jill

POTTS POINT, NSW

SLASHED ROAST LEG OF LAMB

SERVINGS: 6 | PREP TIME: 15 MINS | COOK TIME: 1 HOUR 20 MINS | SKILL LEVEL: 1 (EASY)

INGREDIENTS

3 tbsp roughly chopped
  parsley and/or mint

2 anchovies in oil,
  chopped

3 cloves garlic, crushed

2 tbsp salted capers,
  rinsed

1 tbsp coarsely
  grated lemon rind

80 g soft fresh
  breadcrumbs

3 tbsp extra virgin olive oil,
  plus extra for drizzling

1 leg of lamb, approx. 2 kg

cress or rocket leaves
  for serving

1 lemon, quartered

METHOD

Pre-heat the oven to 220°C.

Combine the parsley, mint, anchovies, garlic, capers, lemon rind and breadcrumbs in a bowl. Add the olive oil and squish the mixture into a soft mushy paste with your hands.

Holding the leg of lamb with its meatiest side on top, cut right through the meat, almost to the bone, at 2 cm intervals. Push the stuffing down between each lamb 'steak', re-shape the meat and tie with kitchen string. Place in a large roasting pan.

Drizzle a little extra olive oil over and bake for 20 minutes. Reduce the heat to 200°C and bake for 1 hour more, then leave to rest for 10 minutes.

Remove the string and carve, parallel to the bone, to form chunky fingers of crisp skin and meat.

Arrange on warm plates, drizzle with the juices from the roasting pan and scatter with cress or rocket. Serve with lemon wedges.

TIP

Don't be scared to slash the lamb meat to the bone. Once stuffed with lemony breadcrumbs, you can tie it all back together again and roast it as normal.

CRASH-HOT POTATOES

SERVINGS: 4 | PREP TIME: 5 MINS | COOK TIME: 1½ HOURS | SKILL LEVEL: 1 (EASY)

INGREDIENTS

8 or more medium-sized
  potatoes, skins on

2 tbsp extra virgin olive oil

1 tbsp thyme and/or
  rosemary sprigs

METHOD

Heat the oven to 200°C.

Scrub the potatoes, pat dry and coat lightly in about 1 tbsp olive oil. Scatter with sea salt, place on the oven rack and bake for 1 hour or until soft inside.

Raise the oven heat to 240°C. Place the potatoes on a baking tray lined with baking paper and punch each potato a few times to flatten it. Push it in at the sides to raise it in the middle, drizzle the remaining olive oil over the top, and scatter generously with sea salt, coarsely ground black pepper, thyme and rosemary.

Bake for 30 minutes or until ridiculously crisp, golden and scorched on the edges, and serve hot.

TIP

The extra-crisp little bits around the edges belong to the cook!

JOSETTE & GEORGE GONTHIER
DAINTREE VANILLA & SPICE

VANILLA & LIME BARBECUED
CHICKEN SKEWERS
SEYCHELLES BANANA FRITTERS

DAINTREE
RAINFOREST,
QLD

Many people think medicine comes from a jar, but it doesn't – it comes from plants. Without them, we would be lost. The vanilla, cinnamon and other tropical plants we grow up here in the Daintree are not just good to eat, they're good for you!

Josette & George

VANILLA & LIME BARBECUED CHICKEN SKEWERS

SERVINGS: 6 | PREP TIME: 15 MINS PLUS 3 HOURS MARINATING
COOK TIME: 10 MINS | SKILL LEVEL: 1 (EASY)

INGREDIENTS

Vanilla and lime salt
1 cup rock salt
zest of 1 lime
¼ tsp vanilla bean paste

800 g chicken breast or
   thigh, cut into 2 cm cubes
olive oil to coat chicken
1½ tbsp vanilla and lime
   salt (see recipe below)
pinch of ground pepper
1 lime

METHOD

For the vanilla and lime salt: in a spice grinder, add in rock salt, lime zest and vanilla bean paste. Blitz until combined. Spread evenly on a baking tray in a low oven (90°C for about an hour) to dry out the salt mix and then store in an airtight container. Delicious on anything from grilled fish to roasted meats.

Soak a big handful of wooden skewers in water for 20 minutes (or for as long as chicken is marinating).

In a large bowl, combine cut chicken, enough olive oil to coat the chicken, vanilla and lime salt, pinch of pepper and the juice of half the lime. Cover and marinate in the fridge for 3 hours.

Pre-heat the barbecue or grill plate to hot. Skewer chicken pieces, and cook on hot barbecue or grill plate for 7–10 minutes or until cooked through. The meat should be juicy, so take care not to overcook. Squeeze the remaining lime half over chicken skewers while they are cooking.

Serve hot with salad, rice or vegetables.

SEYCHELLES BANANA FRITTERS

SERVINGS: 4 | PREP TIME: 10-15 MINS | SKILL LEVEL: 2 (MODERATE)

INGREDIENTS

Batter
250 g plain flour
2½ tbsp beer
50 g sugar
2 whole eggs
2 egg whites

Vanilla and cinnamon sauce
250 g sugar
1 tbsp water
5 tsp dark rum
1 tsp vanilla extract
2½ g ground cinnamon

Fritters
oil for deep-frying
6 bananas
juice of 2–3 limes

METHOD

Prepare the batter: sift flour into a bowl and make a well in the middle. Add beer and sugar to the well, and add the two whole eggs. Mix all the ingredients in the well with a wooden spoon, then gradually stir in the flour to obtain a creamy batter.

In a separate bowl, beat the egg whites until stiff, then add to the batter, stirring gently with a wooden spoon. Cover with a clean cloth and allow to stand at room temperature until you're ready to cook.

Make the sauce: in a heavy-based pot on a medium heat, add the sugar and the water and bring to a simmer. Do not stir the mixture, but you can use a pastry brush moistened with water to brush the sugar crystals that form on the edge of the pot back into the mixture. When the mixture turns a deep caramel colour, remove the pot from the stove and flavour it with rum, vanilla and cinnamon to taste, then set aside.

Make the banana fritters: place oil in a deep pan and heat to 180°C. Peel the bananas, cut in half lengthwise and dip the halves in lime juice to prevent them from oxidising. Dip the banana pieces into batter. Gently lower each battered banana into the oil and fry until golden (about 3–4 minutes each). Set aside on a wire rack or paper towel to drain away the excess oil.

Serve warm with the vanilla and cinnamon sauce.

MATT MORAN

PAN-FRIED BARRAMUNDI WITH A SALAD OF RAW ZUCCHINI & FRESH HERBS

GRILLED PRAWNS WITH OREGANO & LIME

Bondi Beach, to me, is one of the best places on earth.
There's nothing better than finishing work, if you get the
night off, coming down here right on Twilight, having
a swim and then having a cold beer. And when you think
of the beach, you think of fresh Seafood. Barbecued
prawns & barramundi; it's Seafood at its best.
—Matt

NORTH BONDI,
NSW

PAN-FRIED BARRAMUNDI WITH A SALAD OF RAW ZUCCHINI & FRESH HERBS

SERVINGS: 4 | PREP TIME: 15 MINS | COOK TIME: 10 MINS | SKILL LEVEL: 1 (EASY)

INGREDIENTS

2 green zucchini

2 yellow zucchini
  or squash

¼ bunch mint leaves
  (reserve some for garnish)

¼ bunch parsley leaves

Dressing

½ clove garlic,
  finely chopped

zest and juice of 1 lemon
  (reserve some for garnish)

100 ml olive oil

4 x 180 g ocean
  barramundi fillets,
  skin on (I use Cone Bay
  barramundi)

1 tbsp olive oil

sea salt flakes

1 tbsp vegetable
  oil for pan frying

4 tbsp white wine

4 baby zucchini flowers

¼ bunch dill,
  picked into sprigs

METHOD

Using a mandolin, shave the zucchini (or squash) into long thin strips, and place in a bowl with the mint and parsley.

Make the dressing by whisking together the garlic and the lemon zest and juice, then slowly adding the olive oil until combined.

Pat the fillets dry with a paper towel and, using a sharp knife, lightly score the skin enough to go through the skin but not cut into the flesh. Season with olive oil and a good pinch of sea salt.

In a heavy-based frying pan on a medium to high heat, add a tablespoon of vegetable oil and, after a few seconds, place the fillets in the pan, skin-side down. Use a fish slice or spatula to press the fillets flat to the pan to avoid the fillets curling. After 2–3 minutes, or when the skin is crisp and golden, flip the fillets and cook the other side for a further 2 minutes or until just cooked. Remove the fillets from the pan and set aside.

Dress the zucchini and season to taste with salt and freshly ground black pepper. Arrange the salad on the four plates with the fish fillets, and garnish with the dill sprigs, mint leaves and a squeeze of fresh lemon.

GRILLED PRAWNS WITH OREGANO & LIME

SERVINGS: 4 | PREP TIME: 10 MINS | COOK TIME: 3 MINS | SKILL LEVEL: 1 (EASY)

INGREDIENTS

16 large (U6) king prawns

¼ clove garlic, crushed

20 ml chardonnay vinegar

80 ml olive oil,
  plus a little extra

zest and juice of 1 lemon

2 tbsp roughly chopped
  oregano

1 tbsp roughly
  chopped parsley

2 limes, cut in half

METHOD

Pre-heat a grill pan over a high heat.

Split each prawn down the centre of the back and open out, leaving the head and tail intact.

Place the garlic, vinegar, olive oil, lemon zest and juice in a bowl and mix together. Add the oregano, parsley and season with salt and freshly ground black pepper to taste.

Drizzle the prawns with a little olive oil, season with salt and pepper, and place shell side down on the grill pan. Cook for 2 minutes, then turn over and cook for approximately 1 minute on the flesh side. Remove from the heat and place on a serving plate.

To serve, spoon the dressing over the top and place the lime halves alongside.

STEPHANIE ALEXANDER AO

SIMPLEST BEEF STEW

One of the ways to enthuse people who may feel anxious about cooking is to suggest cooking something which is really only about three or four steps. And when it comes out of the oven, it really is so good, that they're going to do it again and again and again.

Stephanie

ABBOTSFORD, VIC

SIMPLEST BEEF STEW

SERVINGS: 4–6 | PREP TIME: 10 MINS | COOK TIME: ABOUT 2 HOURS | SKILL LEVEL: 1 (EASY)

INGREDIENTS

1.5 kg chuck (or blade) steak, cut into large cubes

60 g plain flour

2 tsp best-quality paprika

1 x 400 g can peeled tomatoes in juice

1 glass (250–300 ml) white (or red) wine

1 cup beef stock (or water)

2 onions, diced

2 cloves garlic, sliced

1 stick celery, finely sliced

3 carrots, peeled and cut into chunks

1 fresh (or dried) bay leaf

(DF)

METHOD

Pre-heat oven to 180°C.

Roll beef in flour mixed with paprika (easiest to do this in a plastic bag). Put into a lidded casserole dish that will hold the ingredients comfortably with not too much extra space.

Whizz tomatoes and their juice in a food processor, or crush roughly with a wooden spoon, and add to meat. Add remaining ingredients to casserole and stir. The meat should be almost covered by liquid.

Press a piece of baking paper over contents and cover with lid. Cook in oven, undisturbed, for 2 hours. Taste for seasoning, and add salt and freshly ground black pepper to taste. Check whether meat is tender, and cook longer if necessary – give it another 20 minutes and then check again.

Offer stew with a bowl of yoghurt and maybe a small bowl of sliced pickled dill cucumbers.

IT'S LOVELY SEEING THE SECOND
GENERATION TAKING UP THE REINS
OF THE BUSINESS. ROB'S FATHER SAW
THIS WITH US, WE'RE SEEING IT WITH
OUR KIDS AND WE'VE ALREADY GOT
ANOTHER GENERATION THAT IS
KNEE-HIGH TO A GRASSHOPPER.
HOPEFULLY, IN TIME, THEY TOO WILL
TAKE UP THE REINS.   — SUSAN

HALL,
A.C.T.

THE BRUCE FAMILY
POACHERS PANTRY

SMOKED DUCK BREAST, DUCK LIVER MOUSSE, BUTTERNUT PUMPKIN, TURNIP & BABY CARROTS WITH CHOCOLATE JUS

SMOKED DUCK BREAST, DUCK LIVER MOUSSE, BUTTERNUT PUMPKIN, TURNIP & BABY CARROTS WITH CHOCOLATE JUS

SERVINGS: 4 | PREP TIME: 40 MINS | SKILL LEVEL: 1 (EASY)

INGREDIENTS

4 x 180–250 g smoked duck breasts
1 bunch baby turnips
1 bunch baby carrots
50 g butter

Butternut pumpkin purée

1 medium butternut pumpkin
1 French shallot
100 g butter
1 tbsp chopped fresh oregano
250 ml cream

Chocolate jus

1 French shallot
40 ml olive oil
50 g butter
100 ml port
100 g chocolate powder
200 ml beef stock

Duck liver mousse

300 g duck liver
½ bunch thyme
1 red apple
1 onion
50 g butter
5 tbsp apple juice
100 ml fresh cream
2 tbsp lemon juice

METHOD

Butternut pumpkin puree: peel pumpkin and cut into small cubes. Sauté shallot in butter until soft. Add pumpkin cubes and cook for around 10 minutes on a low heat. Add oregano and cream, and cook until pumpkin is soft (about 10–15 minutes). Blend the purée in a food processor and add salt and pepper to taste.

Chocolate jus: sauté shallot in olive oil and butter until soft. Add port and bring to the boil. Add chocolate powder and beef stock, and bring to the boil. Strain immediately through a fine sieve then reduce to thicken.

Duck liver mousse: clean liver and cut into small strips. Chop thyme and cut apple and onion into small cubes.

Over a low heat, cook apple and onion in butter until soft. Add liver and continue to cook over a low heat for 10 minutes. Add thyme and apple juice, cover and cook for another 5 minutes.

Whip cream. Place duck liver mixture in a food processor and blend until nice and smooth. Allow to cool down to 30°C. Add lemon juice, salt, pepper and cream. Place in the fridge for 2 hours.

To finish: peel turnips and carrots, steam over water until tender (about 10 minutes) and toss in butter with salt to taste.

To serve: gently warm the duck breast in a low oven and then slice diagonally, keeping the pieces together. Spoon some of the pumpkin purée onto a warmed plate, followed by a few of the steamed turnips and carrots. Place a few pieces of the sliced duck meat onto the plate. Finish with a tablespoon of the duck liver mousse and a drizzle of the chocolate jus.

MELBOURNE,
VIC

ANDREW McCONNELL
CUTLER & CO.

MUM'S SWEETCORN FRITTERS
PRAWN & CHICKEN DUMPLINGS
WITH CHILLI & VINEGAR SAUCE
WHITE PEACH, ELDERFLOWER
& FROMAGE BLANC

Cooking at home is hardly a chore when you're cooking with people and for people you love. At home, I never make a meal where I plate five composed separate dishes. Whether it's a roast chicken or a pot of slow cooked meat, it's always served in the middle of the table to eat. It's always a shared table.

MUM'S SWEETCORN FRITTERS

SERVINGS: 4–6 | PREP TIME: 10 MINS | COOK TIME: 20–25 MINS | SKILL LEVEL: 1 (EASY)

INGREDIENTS

1 sweetcorn on the cob
1 x 310 g can creamed corn
1 egg
3 spring onions, thinly sliced
pinch of ground cumin
pinch of ground white
  pepper
3 tbsp self-raising flour
butter and oil, for cooking

METHOD

Plunge the corn cob into a pot of boiling water for 4 minutes. Drain, then cut the kernels from the cob with a sharp knife.

Combine the corn kernels, creamed corn, egg, spring onion and spices in a bowl and whisk well. Sieve the flour into the bowl, along with salt to taste, and beat into a batter.

To test the batter, heat a non-stick frying pan with a teaspoon of oil and a little butter. When the butter has melted, add 1 tablespoon of the batter. Cook over a moderate heat for 2–3 minutes until golden, then flip the fritter and continue to cook for a few minutes more. A little extra flour can be added to the batter if the fritter is not holding together.

Fry the fritters in batches, adding a little extra oil and butter to the pan as necessary.

PRAWN & CHICKEN DUMPLINGS WITH CHILLI & VINEGAR SAUCE

MAKES: APPROX. 20 | PREP TIME: 40 MINS PLUS MARINATING | COOK TIME: 4 MINS
SKILL LEVEL: 2 (MODERATE)

INGREDIENTS

250 g raw prawns, peeled and de-veined
1 tsp egg white
¼ tsp salt
½ tsp tapioca starch
¼ tsp bicarbonate of soda
1 tsp vegetable oil
1 tbsp finely chopped garlic chives
250 g chicken mince
¼ tsp sesame oil

pinch of sugar
¼ tsp salt
1½ tsp soy sauce
¼ tsp fish sauce
pinch of ground white pepper
1 packet wonton wrappers

Chilli & vinegar sauce
1 star anise
¼ tsp coriander seeds

½ stick cinnamon
2 cloves
200 ml water
3½ tbsp Chinese black vinegar
3½ tbsp soy sauce
1½ tbsp sugar
½ cup finely sliced spring onion
½ cup chilli crisp sauce
  (Lao Gan Ma brand is best)

METHOD

Combine the prawns with the egg white, salt, tapioca and bicarbonate and place in the fridge to marinate for 1 hour. Heat the vegetable oil in a small pan and cook the chives for 1 minute, then scrape them into a bowl to cool.

Dice one-third of the marinated prawns and chop the rest finely. Mix with the chicken mince, repeatedly throwing the mixture against the sides of the mixing bowl to form a sticky, cohesive texture. Add the garlic chives, sesame oil, sugar, salt, soy and fish sauces, and white pepper and mix in thoroughly.

Place a rounded teaspoon of the filling in the centre of a wonton wrapper. Moisten the bottom edge of the wrapper with a wet finger. Fold the wrapper in half, towards you, to enclose the filling. Press to seal. Fold the sealed edge back on itself, then lightly moisten one corner of the folded edge. Finally, taking the two ends in your fingers, bring them together with a twisting action, and press them firmly to join. Repeat with remaining filling and wrappers.

To make the chilli and vinegar sauce, toast the spices in a small, dry saucepan until fragrant. Pour in the water, bring to the boil, reduce by half, and cool. Strain, discarding the spices, and stir in the remaining ingredients. Leftover vinegar keeps well in the fridge.

Cook the dumplings for 4 minutes in a large pot of boiling water. Remove them with a slotted spoon and drain. Serve immediately with chilli and vinegar sauce spooned over the top.

WHITE PEACH, ELDERFLOWER & FROMAGE BLANC

SERVINGS: 4 | PREP TIME: 20 MINS PLUS COOLING/MACERATING | SKILL LEVEL: 1 (EASY)

INGREDIENTS

Fromage blanc
175 ml cream
70 g sugar
1 vanilla bean,
  split and scraped
2 leaves gold-strength
  gelatine
350 g fromage blanc
175 ml thickened cream,
  whipped

Peaches
100 g sugar
100 ml water
2 tbsp elderflower cordial
4 perfectly ripe white
  peaches

METHOD

For the fromage blanc: place the cream, sugar, scraped vanilla bean and seeds in a saucepan and bring to a simmer, stirring to dissolve the sugar. In a small bowl, soak the gelatine leaves in cold water for a few minutes until they are soft.

Squeeze the water out of the gelatine and whisk it into the hot cream until it has dissolved. Remove from the heat and leave to cool to room temperature. Remove the vanilla pod. Whisk the fromage blanc to smooth out any lumps, then gradually stir through the cooled vanilla cream. Finally, fold in the whipped cream and refrigerate until set.

To prepare the peaches: bring the sugar and water to a simmer in a small saucepan, then remove from the heat and add the elderflower cordial. Peel and slice the peaches into wedges. Stir a few tablespoons of elderflower syrup through the peaches and leave them to macerate in the fridge for 20 minutes.

To serve, place a large tablespoon of fromage blanc in each bowl, topped with a few pieces of peach and a spoonful of elderflower syrup over the top.

At the end of the week, when we finish on a Sunday afternoon, all we want to do is just cook charcoal chicken, sit in the back yard and knock back a glass of wine. Then we eat dinner together. Sunday is when we sit down as a family. We make a rule not to talk about work, which can be difficult because we work together and food is our lives.

Emma and Scott.

EMMA McCASKILL & SCOTT HUGGINS
PENFOLDS MAGILL ESTATE RESTAURANT

CHARCOAL CHICKEN & CHILLED BROCCOLI
SALAD WITH MISO VINAIGRETTE

MAGILL, SA

CHARCOAL CHICKEN & CHILLED BROCCOLI SALAD WITH MISO VINAIGRETTE

SERVINGS: 4–6 | PREP TIME: 40 MINS PLUS 8 HOURS BRINING
COOK TIME: 2–3 HOURS | SKILL LEVEL: 2 (MODERATE)

INGREDIENTS

4 kg charcoal
1 x 2 kg free-range chicken
3 small, tight heads
  of broccoli
125 g roasted almonds,
  cut widthways

Brine
50 g sugar
150 g salt
3 litres water
4½ g ground black pepper
1 bay leaf
1½ tsp fennel seeds

Vinaigrette
25 ml rice wine vinegar
3 tsp lemon juice
  (½ small lemon)
½ tsp white miso paste
1 clove garlic,
  finely minced
1 tbsp finely
  minced shallot
2 tsp sugar
¾ tsp soy sauce
¼ tsp good Korean
  sesame oil
pinch of salt
50 ml rice bran oil

METHOD

First make up the brine. Dissolve sugar and salt in water in a saucepan on the stovetop. Remove from the heat, add pepper, bay leaf and fennel seeds and allow to cool completely. Add chicken and hold down with a weight, such as a large ceramic plate with a pot on top, to ensure it's fully submerged. Leave to brine for 8 hours, then remove and pat dry.

Light three-quarters of the charcoal in your barbecue and allow to burn for 1 hour.

Attach the chicken to an electric rotisserie and cook over low charcoal heat for 2 hours, adding more charcoal when needed.

While the chicken is cooking, cut broccoli into florets, then halve each floret. Bring a steamer up to a rapid boil and steam broccoli for 1½ minutes. Refresh in salted and iced water. When cold, dry well on paper towel, cover and store in the fridge.

Blend all the vinaigrette ingredients except rice bran oil using a hand-held stick blender. While continuing to blend, slowly add oil until emulsified.

When chicken is ready to carve, combine almonds, broccoli and vinaigrette. Carve chicken into four or eight pieces, choose your favourite piece and enjoy!

TIP

We use a 240-volt rotisserie kit on our charcoal barbecue. You can pick them up from your local hardware store.

JIMMY SHU
HANUMAN

SRI LANKAN FISH MOULI
CHINESE STIR-FRIED KANGKONG
VEGETARIAN CROQUETTES
WITH RED CURRY SAUCE

The market is my second home! It goes back to my childhood, following my Dad to the markets in Sri Lanka where I grew up. There is this vibrancy and you meet and make friends with people. There is an amazing melting pot of cuisines here in Darwin, especially Asian cuisine. Just go the markets, everything you need to cook, all Asian food is there, fresh and alive – Jimmy

DARWIN, NT

SRI LANKAN FISH MOULI
BARRAMUNDI POACHED IN COCONUT CREAM & LEMONGRASS

SERVINGS: 6 | PREP TIME: 25 MINS | SKILL LEVEL: I (EASY)

INGREDIENTS

600 g barramundi fillets, skin
  removed, cut into chunky cubes
2 tbsp vegetable oil
180 g sliced red onion
2 sticks lemongrass, bruised
3 red bird's-eye chillies, bruised
2 sprigs curry leaves
15 g sliced ginger

200 g fresh tomatoes, cut into wedges
600 ml coconut cream
1 tsp turmeric
100 ml water (approx.)
1 tsp salt
1 tsp sugar
fresh curry leaves, to garnish

METHOD

Season the fish with a touch of salt.

Heat oil and stir-fry the onion, lemongrass, chillies, curry leaves and ginger over a medium heat, until the onions are soft. Add the tomato and cook for approximately 5 minutes.

Next, add the coconut cream and turmeric, bring to the boil and lower the heat. Add up to ½ cup of water if too thick. Add salt and sugar, and check the seasoning.

Gently add the fish pieces and poach in the coconut broth for just 6 minutes. Garnish with fresh curry leaves and serve immediately with some steamed rice and a crisp white wine.

CHINESE STIR-FRIED KANGKONG

SERVINGS: 4 | PREP TIME: 10 MINS PLUS SOAKING | SKILL LEVEL: 1 (EASY)

INGREDIENTS

250 g fresh kangkong
  (Asian water spinach), washed
rice bran oil, for stir-frying
3 cloves garlic, peeled
  and lightly crushed
¾ tsp light soy sauce

2 long red chillies, sliced diagonally
  (leave the seeds out if you
  want less heat)
1 big pinch ground white pepper
1½ tsp raw sugar
½ tbsp salted soya beans
  (preserved yellow soya beans)

2 tsp oyster sauce
1½ tsp seasoning sauce (I use Maggi
  Original Seasoning Sauce)
¾ tsp sesame oil
1 tbsp crispy-fried shallots,
  for garnish and flavour

(DF) (V)

METHOD

Soak kangkong for about 30 minutes, then drain. Pluck each leaf separately with stem and attached stalk. Discard fibrous and older part of vegetable. Keep kangkong moist.

Season your wok and bring it to a medium-high heat. This is a fast dish to cook, and your wok needs to be hot enough to seal in the freshness and flavour of the ingredients. When the wok is smoking, add the oil and swirl it around. Add the garlic and, working quickly, keep it constantly moving around the wok for about 20 seconds. Add in the kangkong, soy sauce and chilli and quickly stir everything to combine. Next, toss in the remaining ingredients, except the fried shallots. If possible, place a lid over the wok for a minute to let the kangkong cook in its own steam.

Season with ground white pepper and raw sugar, stir everything together, and transfer it immediately to a serving bowl. Garnish with fried shallots. Perfect as a side dish, or add a fried egg and some steamed jasmine rice for a quick and healthy meal.

VEGETARIAN CROQUETTES WITH RED CURRY SAUCE

SERVINGS: 6 | PREP TIME: 20 MINS | COOK TIME: 30 MINS | SKILL LEVEL: 2 (MODERATE)

INGREDIENTS

Croquettes
200 g paneer, finely diced
40 g carrots, peeled and grated
1½ tsp finely chopped ginger
15 g cashews, chopped coarsely
2 tsp sultanas
3 bunches fresh coriander, chopped
  (reserve some for garnish)
½ red chilli, sliced thinly
100 g potatoes, boiled,
  peeled and mashed
100 g crispy fried onions
100 g besan (gram) flour

25 g green peas
1 tsp salt, or to taste
1 tsp white sugar
½ tsp ground coriander
½ tsp garam masala
½ tsp cumin powder
oil for deep-frying (peanut or
  vegetable oil is best)
coriander leaves, chopped, for garnish

Sauce
75 ml vegetable oil
1 tsp cumin seeds
150 g red onion, diced
½ tsp fresh ginger, finely chopped

1 x 400 g can crushed tomatoes
3 tsp dried fenugreek leaves
1½ tsp cumin powder
50 g butter
1 tsp chilli powder
¼ tsp turmeric
¼ tsp garam masala
1 tsp ground coriander
100 g cashew paste
70 g white sugar
2 tsp salt, or to taste
1 cup cream
½ cup coconut cream

METHOD

Prepare all the croquette ingredients, then combine together and make 12 croquettes. Set aside.

Heat the oil for the sauce in a heavy-based saucepan and add the cumin seeds and stir for 10 seconds. Next, add the red onion and continue stirring for approximately 7 minutes. Then add the ginger and crushed tomatoes and continue stirring over a medium heat. After about 20 minutes check for aromas, and add the remaining ingredients except the cream and coconut cream. Add in the cream and coconut cream just before serving.

Meanwhile, bring a deep-fryer or a large pan of oil to 150–180°C. Deep-fry the croquettes for 5 minutes until golden-brown. Garnish with coriander leaves and serve with the sauce.

 (GF) (V)

ROZELLE,
NSW

ADRIANO ZUMBO

GONE MARBLES CAKE
CUSTARD SPONGE PUDDING

THE MARBLE CAKE WAS MY FIRST
ATTEMPT AT IMPRESSING FRIENDS AT
SCHOOL BY BAKING FOR THEM.
I'D MAKE IT WITH PACKET MIX AND
FOOD COLOURING I NICKED FROM MY
PARENTS' SUPERMARKET! IT REALLY
IS PRICELESS, THE FEELING YOU GET
FROM MAKING SOMEONE HAPPY BY
COOKING FOR THEM.

GONE MARBLES CAKE

SERVINGS: 8–10 | PREP TIME: 1 HOUR PLUS COOLING | COOK TIME: 60–80 MINS
SKILL LEVEL: 2 (MODERATE)

INGREDIENTS

Marble cake batter

150 g unsalted butter,
  at room temperature

240 g caster sugar

180 g egg whites,
  at room temperature

310 g plain flour

5 g baking powder

75 g cornflour

120 g almond meal

100 g crème fraîche

150 g 35%-fat cream

juice and zest of 1 orange

juice and zest of 1 lemon

assorted food colourings

milk or dark chocolate
  to decorate

70% chocolate ganache

340 g dark couverture
  chocolate (70%
  cocoa solids)

400 g 35%-fat cream

140 g unsalted butter

40 g glucose

METHOD

Pre-heat oven to 160°C and grease a 23 cm cake tin.

For the marble cake: in an electric mixing bowl with beater attachment, beat butter and sugar until softened and slightly lightened. Slowly add in egg whites, then add in dry ingredients. Add in crème fraîche and cream, and mix to combine. Lastly add in juices and zests, and continue mixing for 30 seconds until well combined. Divide the mixture into six bowls, 230 g each, and colour each one a different colour, stirring the colour through with a spoon.

Add coloured cake batters to the pre-greased tin in a random mix to form a marble effect. Bake for 60–80 minutes or until the centre is cooked and stable. Remove from oven and leave to cool in the tin for 15 minutes before turning out onto a wire rack to cool completely.

For the ganache: place dark chocolate in a food processor and blitz to make small pieces. In a saucepan place the cream, butter and glucose and heat to 65°C. Pour over the chocolate in the food processor and blitz until smooth and glossy. Pour into a container and cover with plastic wrap touching the surface of the ganache. Place in an air-conditioned cabinet or a cool space to set at room temperature.

To assemble: use a serrated knife to trim the top off the marble cake (it will have formed a slight peak which has cracked open), to make an even-sized cake. Cut the cake horizontally through the middle and separate the halves. Using a scraper, place some of the ganache on the bottom layer – enough to give roughly an 8 mm layer – and spread evenly using a palette knife or spatula. Place the top cake layer on, and cover with more ganache using the palette knife or spatula. Make the entire cake as smooth and neat as you can, covering the whole cake with ganache, then set aside.

For the decoration: for the initiated, spread some tempered chocolate, milk or dark, onto a marble top or a cold tray and leave to 'just' set. Using a palette knife, gently cut through whilst pulling down to form chocolate curls. Arrange the curls to your liking on top of the cake and serve. If you don't know how to temper chocolate, you can make chocolate curls using a vegetable peeler and a block of good-quality store-bought chocolate. At a pinch, you can grate the chocolate as an alternative decoration.

CUSTARD SPONGE PUDDING

SERVINGS: 6 | PREP TIME: 45 MINS | COOK TIME: 30 MINS | SKILL LEVEL: 2 (MODERATE)

INGREDIENTS

softened butter for
  greasing pudding moulds

Custard
(makes approx. 880 g)
2 vanilla beans
350 g milk
150 g 35%-fat cream
180 g egg yolks
125 g caster sugar
30 g cornflour
50 g unsalted butter

Sponge cake
100 g plain flour
100 g cornflour
290 g egg whites
180 g caster sugar
160 g egg yolks
10 g honey
  (I use Tasmanian
  leatherwood honey)
200 g custard
fresh raspberries
  and mango slices
soft eating liquorice

METHOD

Pre-heat oven to 140°C. Grease small pudding moulds with a little softened butter.

Split vanilla beans, add to milk and cream in a medium-sized saucepan and bring to the boil, stirring occasionally. Mix together egg yolks, sugar and cornflour in a bowl. Pour a third of the hot milk into the egg mixture to temper it, stir to combine completely, then pour back into the saucepan with remaining hot liquid. Return to a medium heat and, constantly stirring with a whisk, cook until it reaches 65°C. Remove from the heat and add in butter until combined. Place 60 g of custard in the bottom of each small pudding mould, reserving the remainder.

Sieve plain flour and cornflour together. In an electric mixer fitted with the whisk attachment, place the egg whites and caster sugar and whip until medium peaks are formed. Add in the egg yolks and honey, mix through, then remove from mixer and fold through sifted flours.

Place 350 g of the custard in a bowl and fold through the sponge mixture.

Divide the mixture into 150 g per mould, place the pudding moulds in a roasting tray and fill halfway up with water. Bake for around 30 minutes or until sponge is cooked and stable. Remove from oven and de-mould onto a plate. Spoon some of the remaining custard over.

Decorate with fresh raspberries and mango slices, and finish by grating some soft eating liquorice over the dish using a microplane.

Someone asked me recently "What makes having a family so special?" & I think it's one of those things you don't really know how special it is untill you have one of your own. Once you do, you fight against it to go back to what you were before but there's something amazing that happens that brings you together. I think one of the best things about having a family is the coming together & sharing of food. The food can be simple, but it's the people around you that creates the memory not just the food itself.

NORTHCOTE, VIC

MATT WILKINSON

I HATE PESTO
MANGO & COCONUT ICE-BLOCKS

I HATE PESTO

MAKES: APPROX. *500* ML | PREP TIME: *5* MINS | SKILL LEVEL: I (EASY)

When I was growing up, my dad used to make us pasta with pesto from a jar and I hated it! These days, we grow basil in huge amounts at home and my kids absolutely love it.

INGREDIENTS

2 big handfuls basil leaves, washed

1 tbsp toasted pine nuts, plus extra untoasted pine nuts for garnishing

2 tbsp finely grated Parmesan, with extra for garnishing

juice of ½ lemon

salt and pepper

½ cup olive oil

METHOD

This is the basic pesto recipe we use – put it all in the blender and blitz until smooth but with a few small chunks. Garnish with the extra pine nuts and Parmesan.

TIPS

The pasta we serve with this does not resemble anything like the penne from my childhood years. I love different types of pasta shapes – seriously, an extra few dollars for a good dried pasta and some different shapes makes all the difference and is fun for the kids. I have provided a list below of some of the different shapes we like with pesto:

- bucatini (like a thicker spaghetti, but hollow)

- matriciani (similar to bucatini but folded over rather than a tube)

- trofie (torpedo-shaped spirals)

- spaghettoni (extra-long spaghetti)

- orecchiette (little ears)

- trecce dell'orto ('braids of the garden'; tight twists in five colours)

See the cooking instructions on the packet – I generally have no idea!

MANGO & COCONUT ICE-BLOCKS

MAKES: 10 | PREP TIME: 10 MINS PLUS FREEZING | SKILL LEVEL: 1 (EASY)

INGREDIENTS

4 medium mangoes
270 ml coconut cream
  (or vanilla yoghurt
  or plain yoghurt)
2 tsp honey

METHOD

Peel the mangoes and remove the flesh from the seeds. Discard skin and seeds, and roughly chop the mango flesh. Put the mango with the coconut cream and honey into a food processor or blender and blitz to a smooth purée. Pour immediately into a popsicle tray, insert a lollipop stick into each and freeze overnight.

TIP

The quantity and flavour can vary depending on what's growing in your garden (or what you picked from the neighbours' tree). Peaches and nectarines, pineapples and summer berries all work well. Adjust the coconut cream so that you have a ratio of 50/50 fruit to coconut cream.

CLAYTON DONOVAN

OYSTERS WITH FINGER LIME, CARROT FOAM & AVOCADO CREAM
KANGAROO SAN CHOY BAU

The women in my family form a huge part of what I know about my culture, and I've passed what I know onto my kids. It's important that Australians know and consume our indigenous foods. Not only are they sustainable, but who knows what we'll discover the more we pay attention.
- Clayton

NAMBUCCA HEADS, NSW

OYSTERS WITH FINGER LIME, CARROT FOAM & AVOCADO CREAM

SERVINGS: 2 | PREP TIME: 30 MINS | SKILL LEVEL: 2 (MODERATE)

INGREDIENTS

200 ml carrot juice (from about 6 carrots)

1½ tsp lecithin

2 avocados

2 tbsp lemon juice

100 ml cream

12 shucked Nambucca River oysters

2 finger limes

METHOD

Warm the carrot juice to blood temperature, and remove from the stove. Add the lecithin and stir. Season to taste with salt and pepper. Set aside.

Mash the avocados with the lemon juice. Push the mixture through a sieve. Whip the cream just under soft peak stage. Fold the cream into the avocado mixture, then season to taste.

Squeeze out the liquid from the finger limes and remove the seeds.

Lightly pulse the carrot mixture until foam rises, then put aside to settle.

Place the avocado mixture on top of each oyster. Put the finger limes on top, then spoon the carrot foam on top of this.

KANGAROO SAN CHOY BAU
SAVOURY LETTUCE CUPS

SERVINGS: 4 | PREP TIME: 20 MINS | SKILL LEVEL: 1 (EASY)

INGREDIENTS

½ red capsicum, deseeded

½ yellow capsicum, deseeded

1 tbsp sesame oil, for frying

1 tbsp Brookfarm Lime & Chilli Infused Macadamia Oil, for frying

25 g brown onion, finely diced

1 large clove garlic, chopped

25 g celery, diced

1 thumb-sized piece ginger, peeled and finely grated

600 g kangaroo mince

1 tbsp ground native bush tomato

1 tbsp soy sauce

1 tbsp oyster sauce

1 tbsp fish sauce

20 g red onion, finely diced

30 g snow peas, finely sliced

30 g spring onion, sliced thinly

½ bunch coriander, chopped

8–10 large leaves mint, finely sliced

8–10 large Vietnamese mint leaves, finely sliced

12 lettuce cups

½ red chilli and ½ green chilli (or to taste), finely sliced

1 lime, quartered

METHOD

Dice most of the capsicum, and thinly slice the rest for garnish.

Heat a large frying pan over a moderate heat, add sesame and lime and chilli oil. Add the brown onion, garlic, celery, the diced red and yellow capsicum and the ginger. Cook until the onion and garlic have softened.

Add the kangaroo mince and stir. Brown the meat.

Add the bush tomato, soy sauce, oyster sauce and fish sauce. Taste for fish sauce seasoning and add more if necessary.

Remove from the heat. Add the red onion, remaining capsicum, and snow peas and mix through. Add the spring onion, coriander, mint and Vietnamese mint.

Place the mixture into the lettuce cups and serve with the sliced chillies and lime quarters.

KATRINA RYAN
THE GOLDEN PIG FOOD & WINE SCHOOL

DAD'S SCRAMBLED EGGS WITH SALMON ROE & HOME-MADE SOUR CREAM
SUGAR-CURED SALMON CROSTINI WITH GOAT'S FETA & SALSA

My Stepmother is a fantastic cook, and scrambled eggs is my Dad's dish. He doesn't cook much else but he's very good at scrambled eggs. As he says, it's all in the timing. You have to get it on the toast and out to the table at the right time.

- Katrina

NEWSTEAD, QLD

DAD'S SCRAMBLED EGGS WITH SALMON ROE & HOME-MADE SOUR CREAM

SERVINGS: 6 | PREP TIME: 20 MINS PLUS CULTURING | SKILL LEVEL: 1 (EASY)

INGREDIENTS

Home-made sour cream (makes 300 ml)
300 ml cream
⅛ tsp Flora Danica culture (may be purchased online and kept in the freezer)

Scrambled eggs
12 free-range eggs
300 ml cream
1½ tbsp butter

To serve
100 ml home-made sour cream (see recipe)
6 tsp salmon roe
1 tbsp chopped chives
1 tbsp dill sprigs

METHOD

Home-made sour cream: heat the cream to 35°C in a small saucepan. Whisk in the Flora Danica, cover with a lid and leave for 24 hours at room temperature. The cream will thicken and taste pleasantly sour. Refrigerate until ready to use. Will keep for up to three weeks.

Scrambled eggs: whisk together the eggs and cream in a bowl. Heat the butter in a frying pan until it starts to bubble, and add the egg mix. Cook over a low to moderate heat, stirring occasionally, allowing the eggs to set and form large curds. Don't over-stir! Season with salt and pepper when nearly cooked.

Serve eggs immediately, topped with sour cream, salmon roe, chives and dill on your choice of toasted, buttered bread.

SUGAR-CURED SALMON CROSTINI WITH GOAT'S FETA & SALSA

SERVINGS: 6 | PREP TIME: 30 MINS PLUS CURING | COOK TIME: 45 MINS | SKILL LEVEL: 1 (EASY)

INGREDIENTS

Sugar-cured salmon
500 g salmon fillet
½ cup chopped dill leaves
⅓ cup caster sugar
⅓ cup table salt

Salsa
1 red capsicum
olive oil for drizzling
3 large ripe tomatoes
10 Kalamata olives, pitted
3 tbsp chopped chives
⅓ cup chopped dill leaves
juice of 1 small lemon
4 tbsp extra virgin olive oil

To serve
6 thick slices artisan bread
butter to taste
6 tbsp Meredith Dairy marinated goat's feta
extra virgin olive oil for drizzling
6 lemon wedges

METHOD

Remove the pin-bones and skin from the salmon. Press the dill leaves onto the salmon. Mix sugar and salt together and cover the salmon all over with the mixture. Cover with plastic wrap, place the salmon in a container and refrigerate for 24 hours. When cured, lightly wash salmon in cold water and pat dry with paper towels. Slice very thinly.

Pre-heat oven to 165°C. Place the capsicum on a baking tray and drizzle with olive oil. Bake for 45 minutes, turning once or twice, then remove and allow to cool. Hold capsicum stalk down and pull the stalk and seeds out. Remove skin and cut flesh into thin strips. Finely dice tomatoes and roughly chop olives. Mix all salsa ingredients together and season to taste with sea salt and freshly ground black pepper.

Toast bread and spread it with butter. Roughly spread feta over each piece of toast. Top with a large spoonful of salsa and then drape slices of salmon over. Top with a little more salsa and finish with a drizzle of olive oil, a good grind of pepper and a lemon wedge on the side.

LYNDEY MILAN OAM

MEATLOAF WITH ITALIAN FLAVOURS
MY ULTIMATE MACARONI & CHEESE

Comfort food is, of course, different to different people & it is especially different for different cultures. Personally, I think you should eat comfort food with one hand. Nothing formal, just a fork will do.

Lyndey

WAVERTON,
NSW

MEATLOAF WITH ITALIAN FLAVOURS

SERVINGS: 6 | PREP TIME: 15 MINS | COOK TIME: 1 HOUR | SKILL LEVEL: 1 (EASY)

INGREDIENTS

250 g Italian sausages

1 large (350 g) red capsicum, chopped finely

1 large (200 g) brown onion, chopped finely

4 cloves garlic, chopped finely

500 g beef mince

100 g sliced salami or chorizo, coarsely chopped

½ cup good-quality pitted black olives, halved

¾ cup (50 g) fresh breadcrumbs

⅓ cup (80 ml) good-quality barbecue sauce

2 eggs, beaten lightly

¼ cup flat-leaf parsley, chopped finely

125 g cherry tomatoes, halved

1 x 400 g can diced tomatoes

basil leaves, for garnish

salad or seasonal green vegetables, to serve

METHOD

Pre-heat oven to 200°C.

Line a 1.5 litre loaf tin (e.g. 20 cm x 12 cm x 8 cm) with plastic wrap to mould meatloaf in. Using baking paper, line a baking tray big enough to hold the loaf tin (a lamington tray is perfect).

Remove sausages from their skins, crumble and, in a large bowl, combine with capsicum, onion, garlic, beef mince, salami or chorizo, olives, breadcrumbs, barbecue sauce, egg and parsley. Press this mixture tightly into the loaf tin, then turn it out onto the baking dish and remove the loaf tin which has acted as a mould. Combine cherry and canned tomatoes and pour evenly over the meatloaf.

Bake meatloaf, uncovered, for about 1 hour or until cooked through. If the cherry tomatoes start to burn, cover with tinfoil. Stand for 10 minutes before cutting. Serve with salad or steamed vegetables, as desired.

MY ULTIMATE MACARONI & CHEESE

SERVINGS: 4 AS A LUNCH OR SIDE DISH | PREP TIME: 20 MINS
COOK TIME: 20 MINS | SKILL LEVEL: 1 (EASY)

INGREDIENTS

300 g dried macaroni

20 g butter

1 leek, finely sliced

2 cloves garlic,
  finely chopped

200 ml milk

300 ml cream

1–2 tsp Dijon mustard,
  to taste

pinch of nutmeg

1 egg, lightly beaten

½ cup (100 g) ricotta

1½ cups (180 g) grated
  Australian cloth-bound
  cheddar

½ cup (100 g) chopped
  Australian blue cheese
  (creamy style)

1 tbsp chives, finely chopped

4–6 slices (60 g) prosciutto,
  torn into small pieces

½ cup (35 g) panko
  breadcrumbs

METHOD

Pre-heat oven to 200°C (180°C fan-forced). Grease a medium (2-litre) casserole or baking dish, or four individual dishes.

Add macaroni to a large saucepan of salted boiling water, stir well, bring back to the boil and cook according to directions or until al dente (approximately 10 minutes). Drain well.

Meanwhile, melt butter over a medium heat in a medium saucepan, add leek and garlic, and cook for 3 minutes or until soft. Add milk, cream, mustard and nutmeg, mix well and bring to the boil. Remove from the heat and whisk in egg, ricotta, 1 cup cheddar cheese and all the blue cheese. Stir until combined. Gently fold in macaroni and chives. Season to taste with salt and pepper.

Pour macaroni mixture into prepared dish (or dishes). Combine prosciutto, breadcrumbs and remaining cheddar cheese and sprinkle over macaroni. Bake for 15 minutes (or 10 minutes for individual dishes) or until the sauce is bubbling and the top is golden. Remove and rest for 5 minutes. Serve with a green salad, if desired.

TIP

I like a tube-shaped pasta for this style of recipe, so use elbow macaroni or penne.

PIERRE KHODJA

ROASTED BABY BARRAMUNDI WITH SAUTÉED CALAMARI & VERMICELLI
STEAMED LAMB SHOULDER WITH APRICOT & CINNAMON
COUSCOUS WITH PEAS & MINT

For me, if you eat properly and you look after your self – and I see it in North africa where I was born and the Arab world – you'll live for a hundred years, if you eat well, you live well –

Pierre – KHODJA

MORNINGTON
PENINSULA,
VIC

ROASTED BABY BARRAMUNDI WITH SAUTÉED CALAMARI & VERMICELLI

SERVINGS: 2 | PREP TIME: 40 MINS | SKILL LEVEL: 2 (MODERATE)

INGREDIENTS

4 tbsp olive oil

1 large clove garlic, chopped

½ red chilli, chopped

1 small onion, diced

250 g cherry tomatoes

½ tsp ground cumin

1 tbsp sumac

1 tbsp raisins,
  soaked in hot water

1 tbsp pomegranate molasses

1 cup vegetable stock or water

200 g vermicelli, soaked in
  hot water for 3 minutes

1 tbsp chopped parsley

1 tbsp chopped coriander leaves,
  plus extra leaves for garnish

1 whole barramundi
  (about 500 g), cleaned

1 medium-sized fresh calamari,
  cleaned and sliced

squeeze of lemon

METHOD

Pre-heat the oven to 180°C.

Heat 1½ tablespoons of olive oil in a frying pan. Add garlic and cook for 1 minute, then add chilli and onion. Cook for 5 minutes, then add cherry tomatoes, cumin and sumac, and cook for another 5 minutes on a low heat. Then add drained raisins and pomegranate molasses and cook for 2 minutes.

Add vegetable stock or water and reduce by half, then add drained vermicelli. Season with salt and pepper, add parsley and coriander, and reduce to a thick consistency. Keep warm.

In a hot ovenproof frying pan, heat another 1½ tablespoons of olive oil and sear the barramundi until brown on both sides, then place in the oven and cook for 8 minutes.

Sauté the calamari in remaining olive oil for 2 minutes, until brown. Place the vermicelli mixture on a serving plate, take the barramundi out of the oven and place on top of the vermicelli. Garnish with calamari and coriander leaves, and squeeze lemon juice on top.

STEAMED LAMB SHOULDER WITH APRICOT & CINNAMON

SERVINGS: 4 | PREP TIME: 40 MINS | COOK TIME: 2½ HOURS | SKILL LEVEL: 1 (EASY)

INGREDIENTS

1.25 kg lamb shoulder, off the bone
1½ tbsp ground cumin
1 tbsp coarse sea salt
½ tsp ground black pepper
1 pinch saffron threads
1 tbsp olive oil
8 cloves garlic
½ bunch parsley stalks
½ bunch coriander stalks (reserve leaves to serve)

Apricot sauce
1 large shallot, sliced
1 tbsp ghee
4 whole dried apricots
4 whole dried prunes
1 whole stick cinnamon
1 tbsp red wine vinegar
1 tsp brown sugar
1 cup orange juice

To serve
oil for frying
coriander leaves

METHOD

To prepare the lamb, wipe with a damp cloth and then make small cuts into the meat on both sides.

Combine the cumin, sea salt, pepper, saffron and olive oil and bring together to form a paste. Rub this mixture into the lamb, then cover and leave to marinate for 30 minutes to allow the flavours to penetrate.

Place the lamb on a large square of muslin or baking paper, with the fat side up. Top with half of the garlic cloves and tie the muslin or baking paper over the top.

Fill the base of a couscoussier or large steamer to three-quarters full. Cover and bring to the boil.

Line the base of the steamer basket with the parsley and coriander stalks, together with remaining garlic. Place the lamb on top and put lid on firmly. Reduce the heat and steam for 2–2½ hours. It is important not to remove the lid for the first hour of cooking. When cooked, the lamb should be beautifully tender.

Meanwhile, make the apricot sauce. Sauté the shallot in the ghee until soft. Add the fruit and cinnamon stick and cook for 3 minutes. Add red wine vinegar and deglaze the pan, stirring to incorporate everything. Add sugar and orange juice, and cook for 30 minutes or until it becomes a sauce.

To serve, heat some oil in a large pan, brown the lamb on each side and serve with cumin and sea salt on the side. Warm apricot sauce and pour over the lamb shoulder, garnish with coriander leaves and serve. It may be served with couscous.

COUSCOUS WITH PEAS & MINT

SERVINGS: 4 | PREP TIME: 20 MINS | SKILL LEVEL: 1 (EASY)

INGREDIENTS

300 g pearl (Israeli) couscous
4 tbsp olive oil
2 bunches asparagus
3 cups fresh peas
2 shallots, diced
1 bunch flat-leaf parsley, washed and chopped
½ bunch mint, washed and chopped
zest and juice of 1 large lemon

METHOD

Cook couscous in boiling water according to instructions on packet.

Dress with 2 tablespoons of olive oil and separate with a fork to prevent the pearls sticking together.

Peel and blanch asparagus in boiling water for 2 minutes, then refresh in iced water. Repeat this process with the peas.

Mix couscous, asparagus, peas, shallots and herbs together and dress with lemon zest and juice, remaining oil, and sea salt and freshly ground black pepper to taste.

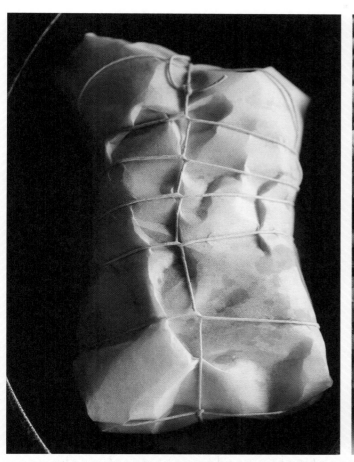

DAVE CAMPBELL
WHARF RD RESTAURANT & BAR

TIRADITO SALAD OF OCEAN TROUT & SCALLOPS

BARBECUED WAGYU SKIRT STEAK WITH CHIMICHURRI

NO-BAKE CHOCOLATE RIPPLE CAKE WITH FRESH BERRIES

The best thing we could have done was to move to the country so we could spend more time with our young girls. Children love to be involved in anything their parents want to do and there are so many things they can do that make them feel like they're contributing. Those times create memories for them which will last forever.

Dave & Nicole

BROUGHTON VILLAGE, NSW

TIRADITO SALAD OF OCEAN TROUT & SCALLOPS
CEVICHE SEAFOOD SALAD

SERVINGS: 6 | PREP TIME: 20 MINS | SKILL LEVEL: 1 (EASY)

INGREDIENTS

Dressing
100 ml ají amarillo paste (you can buy this from online retailers)
100 ml extra virgin olive oil
70 ml lime juice

Salad
600 g ocean trout, skinned and pin-boned
400 g Queensland scallops, roe removed
½ bunch coriander
½ bunch fennel tops

100 g broad beans, blanched and second skin removed
50 ml Shiro Shoyu soy sauce (light and a little less salty in flavour)
salt to taste (I use Murray River pink salt)

(DF)

METHOD

The dressing: combine ají amarillo, olive oil and lime juice together in a bowl and stir with a whisk until combined.

The salad: slice ocean trout as you would for sashimi. Place a scallop on a board, lay your knife flat, raise it about 2 mm and gently slice through the scallop. Lift up the rest of the scallop and leave the slice on the chopping board. Repeat with remaining scallops until all are cut into thin slices.

Arrange slices of trout and scallop on the plate. Pick coriander leaves and give them a quick rough chop. Scatter coriander, fennel tops and broad beans over the trout and scallop.

Drizzle dressing generously over the salad. Lightly drizzle Shoyu over the salad and finish with the salt. The salt adds texture to the dish; if you can't get pink salt then Maldon or kosher salt will do.

TIP

You can use your favourite fish for this recipe and slice it as you would for sashimi. You can always ask your fishmonger to slice it for you, and then all you have to do is put it on a plate and dress it.

BARBECUED WAGYU SKIRT STEAK WITH CHIMICHURRI

SERVINGS: 6 | PREP TIME: 5 MINS PLUS RESTING | COOK TIME: 5–6 MINS | SKILL LEVEL: 1 (EASY)

INGREDIENTS

1 kg Wagyu skirt steak, trimmed (inside skirt is my favourite)
2 lemons, cut into wedges

Chimichurri
2 cups coriander leaves
1 cup flat-leaf parsley leaves

1 cup mint leaves
1 cup chopped green shallot
4 cloves garlic
2 long red chillies, stems removed

500 ml virgin olive oil
80 ml lemon juice
1 tbsp sweet paprika
100 ml red wine vinegar
salt to taste

 (DF) (GF)

METHOD

Cut skirt steak into six equal portions. It's very rich, so you don't need much. Season well with salt and allow to come to room temperature. Meanwhile, heat up your barbecue, and combine all chimichurri ingredients in a food processor and blend until smooth.

Cook meat on the hot barbecue until medium-rare. It should take 2–3 minutes on each side. Spoon some of the chimichurri over the top of the steak and remove from the barbecue. Cover with tinfoil and place in a warm spot to rest for 5 minutes.

Put any remaining chimichurri in a jar with a tight lid and place in the fridge. It will last a month if you don't eat it first.

NO-BAKE CHOCOLATE RIPPLE CAKE
WITH FRESH BERRIES

SERVINGS: 6 | PREP TIME: 10 MINS PLUS STANDING | SKILL LEVEL: 1 (EASY)

INGREDIENTS

1 litre cream
  (local and organic,
  if possible)

2 tsp vanilla extract

1 x 250 g pack Arnott's
  Choc Ripple biscuits
  (Arnott's Chocolate
  Coated Teddy Bear
  biscuits work well too)

1 x 200 g block dark
  chocolate (70% cocoa)

1 punnet blueberries

1 punnet raspberries

METHOD

This needs to be prepared 12 hours in advance. Have a serving plate ready to go, rectangular works the best.

Combine cream and vanilla in a mixer with a whisk, and whip to soft peaks. Spoon a tablespoon of cream onto a biscuit. Place another biscuit on top of the cream to make a sandwich. Place the biscuit sandwich on its side at the end of the serving plate. Take another biscuit and place a spoon of cream on, then add that biscuit to the one on the platter. Repeat with the whole packet.

Spoon cream on top of the biscuit log. Use a spatula or spoon to cover the whole log with cream, including the ends. Place in the fridge overnight.

To serve, use a vegetable peeler to peel along the side of the chocolate block, creating chocolate shavings. Scatter the berries over the log and finish with chocolate shavings. Cut the log on an angle with a sharp knife when serving.

JOCK ZONFRILLO
ORANA

LAMB, BEETROOTS, POTATOES & PEAS WITH EUCALYPTUS OIL

I'm from an Italian Scottish family....
Our Italian family dinners were typically
hands everywhere, yelling & shouting & sauce
up the walls - our staff dinners are
no different!! We're at work eighteen
hours a day, & a staff meal is a great
opportunity once a day for everyone
to chew the fat.

Jock

ADELAIDE, SA

LAMB, BEETROOTS, POTATOES & PEAS WITH EUCALYPTUS OIL

SERVINGS: 4 | PREP TIME: 45 MINS | COOK TIME: APPROX. 1 HOUR | SKILL LEVEL: 2 (MODERATE)

INGREDIENTS

2 x lamb knuckles
   (I use black-faced
   Suffolk lamb)

4 medium-sized beetroots

4 waxy, yellow-fleshed
   potatoes, about the
   same size and shape

50 ml grapeseed oil

100 g butter

2 cloves garlic,
   peeled and halved

4 sprigs thyme

2 sprigs rosemary

500 g fresh peas

100 ml jus or basic
   stock-based sauce

Eucalyptus oil

handful Eucalyptus
   brunnea leaves plus extra
   for smoking (if you have
   access to one of these
   trees, brilliant; if not,
   substitute with parsley)

150 ml grapeseed oil

METHOD

Cut the lamb knuckles in half lengthways and clean off any extra sinew (you can ask your butcher to do this for you). They can be cooked two ways: sous vide in a vacuum-sealed bag at 52°C for 1 hour or slow-smoked at about 130°C for about 1 hour. If cooking sous vide, let the meat rest for around 10 minutes before finishing (see below). If smoking, I recommend a temperature-controlled electric smoker, and allow the meat to rest for 20 minutes before finishing.

Meanwhile, pre-heat the oven to 150°C and bake the whole beetroots until wrinkled and soft, around an hour or so. Do not wrap them in anything, just place them directly onto a baking tray and into the oven. Once cool enough to handle, peel them and set aside for later. Leave the oven on (or re-heat it when you are ready to serve).

While the beetroots are in the oven, quarter the potatoes lengthways and peel (I use a small paring knife and carefully peel the skin off to give a banana-like shape to the peeled potato and then cut a small indent in the straight side so that the potato pieces are an even thickness the whole way around). Heat the oil in a heavy-based frying pan and test the temperature by throwing a piece of potato in – there should be an instant sizzle and the potato will start to colour quickly. Throw the rest of the potatoes in and roll around until coloured and not sticking. At this stage the butter needs to be thrown in, one small piece at a time. Reduce the heat slightly and allow the butter to foam around the potatoes – there should be enough to submerge them. Throw in the garlic and the thyme and rosemary sprigs. The potatoes will be nicely golden by now. Continue cooking until soft in the centre, being careful to control the heat at all times. Once cooked, leave in a warm spot, in the butter, until all the other ingredients are ready.

Pod the peas and blanch them for 2 minutes in boiling water, then refresh in ice-water before straining and setting aside.

For the eucalyptus oil: throw the leaves and the oil in a blender and blend on high for 5 minutes. Pass oil through a coffee filter paper and set aside. If you are making parsley oil, blanch parsley briefly in boiling water and squeeze to remove excess water. Allow to dry until it is dry to the touch, then continue with blending and straining as for eucalyptus oil.

Throw the beetroots back in the oven to warm through. Once the lamb has rested, finish off by sealing it on the barbecue, preferably over an open flame so that you can throw a few eucalyptus leaves underneath to smoke the lamb nicely. Once sealed, allow to rest for a few minutes before carving. Toss the peas in a little butter over a medium heat with salt and white pepper.

To serve, place the beetroots first, one on each plate. Drain the potatoes a little on paper towel and place next to the beetroot. Carve the lamb, season and place on the plate, and sprinkle the peas over the top. Drizzle the eucalyptus or parsley oil over the top, along with a spoonful of jus to finish.

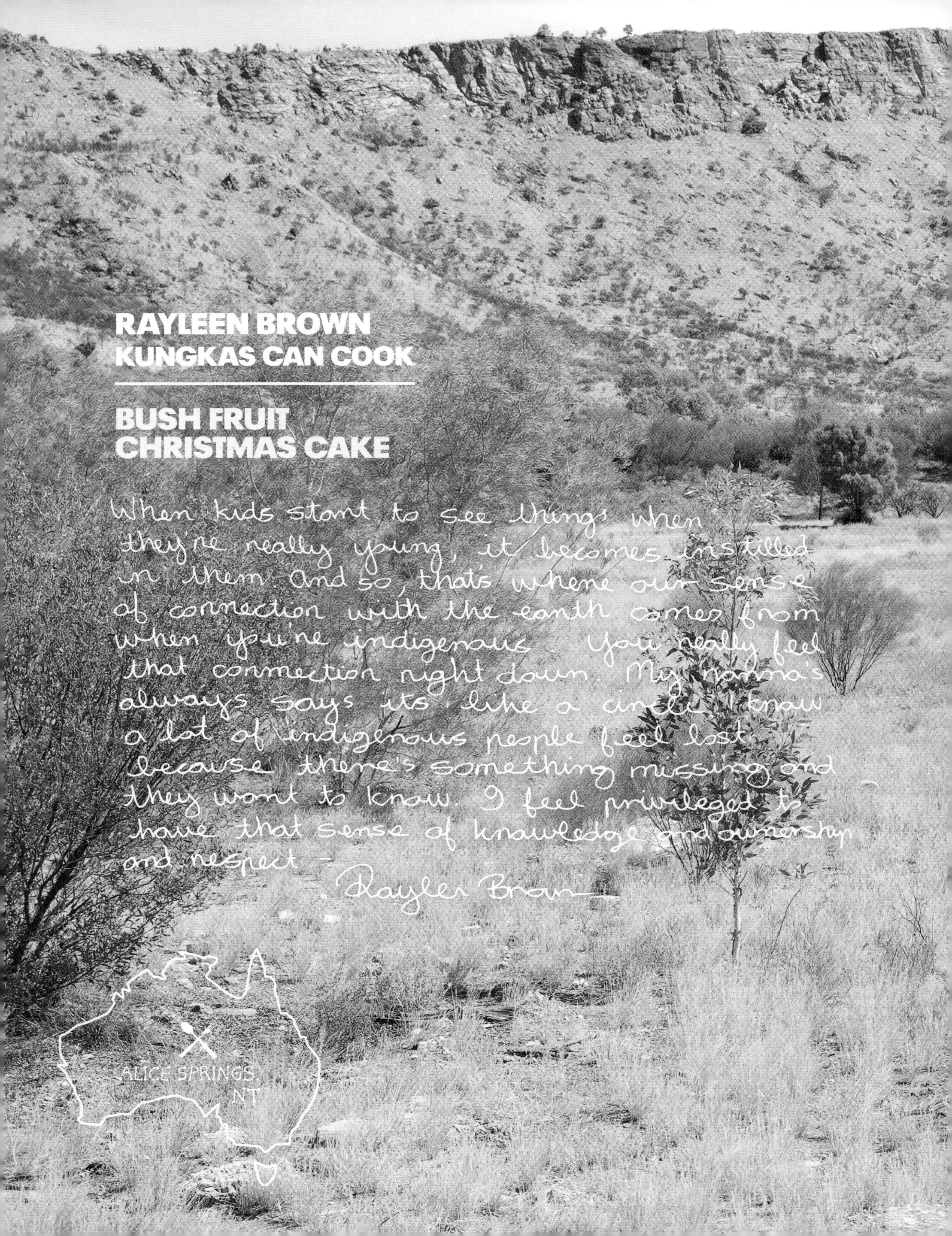

RAYLEEN BROWN
KUNGKAS CAN COOK

BUSH FRUIT
CHRISTMAS CAKE

When kids start to see things when they're really young, it becomes instilled in them and so, that's where our sense of connection with the earth comes from when you're indigenous. You really feel that connection right down. My nanna's always says its like a circle. I know a lot of indigenous people feel lost because there's something missing and they want to know. I feel privileged to have that sense of knowledge and ownership and respect.

— Rayleen Brown

ALICE SPRINGS
NT

BUSH FRUIT CHRISTMAS CAKE

SERVINGS: 12 | PREP TIME: 30 MINS PLUS STANDING
COOK TIME: 3 HOURS | SKILL LEVEL: 1 (EASY)

INGREDIENTS

1½ cups sultanas

½ cup coarsely
chopped raisins

½ cup coarsely chopped
pitted dates

2½ cups fresh or frozen
quandong, de-seeded

½ cup chopped glazed
apricots

¼ cup quandong jam

¾ cup Cointreau or other
orange liqueur

250 g butter, softened

¾ cup firmly packed
brown sugar

2 eggs

2 cups plain flour

1 tsp mixed spice

1½ cups macadamia nuts

1 tsp ground bush tomato

1 tsp ground pepperberry

1 tsp wattleseed, toasted
and ground

Decoration

1 cup apricot jam

1½ cups water

500 g fresh or frozen
quandong halves

METHOD

Combine fruit, jam and liqueur in a large bowl and mix well. Cover and stand overnight or for several days, stirring mixture occasionally.

Pre-heat oven to 140°C. Line the base and sides of a deep 20 cm round cake tin with baking paper, allowing 5 cm to extend above the tin.

Beat butter and sugar in a small bowl with an electric beater, until creamy. Add eggs one at a time, beating until just combined between each egg. Add butter mix to fruit mixture and stir well. Stir in sifted flour and mixed spice, then macadamias, bush tomato, pepperberry and wattleseed.

Spread mixture evenly into cake tin. Bake for 3 hours or until a skewer inserted into the centre comes out clean.

Decoration: place jam and water in a small saucepan, bring to the boil and simmer uncovered until reduced to half. Strain into a bowl, discarding pulp. Allow to cool. Thaw quandongs if frozen.

Quickly toss quandong halves in cooled glaze. Carefully place halves on top of cooled cake. This is a very sticky job, but take your time.

CHEONG LIEW OAM

CHAR KWAY TEOW
BEEF RENDANG

I learnt to cook from my mum and grandma. As a kid, I had to be part of the kitchen team to wash the rice, build the fire, wash the vegetables, even just to be the stirrer when mum said "Don't let it stick!" My style of cooking is I improvise. That means you're putting your soul and heart into the dish, as opposed to one teaspoon of this or a cup of that.

Cheong

UNLEY, SA

CHAR KWAY TEOW
WOK-FRIED RICE NOODLES

SERVINGS: 2–3 | PREP TIME: 30 MINS | SKILL LEVEL: 1 (EASY)

INGREDIENTS

2 tbsp light soy sauce

1 tbsp thick dark soy sauce

2 tbsp vegetable oil

2 cloves garlic, finely chopped

1 lap cheong (Chinese sausage), thinly sliced

6 raw prawns, peeled and de-veined

100 g fish cake, sliced (see tip below)

400 g fresh flat rice noodles

1 tsp ground white pepper

1 tsp vinegared chilli sauce (optional)

1 tbsp lard crisps

1 egg

handful of bean sprouts

handful of garlic chives, cut into 5 cm lengths

METHOD

Combine light soy and thick dark soy sauces with 2 tablespoons of water and mix well.

In a wok, heat vegetable oil over a high heat, then add garlic and lap cheong and stir-fry for 1 minute. Add prawns and fish cake slices and stir-fry for a further minute until the prawns are cooked.

Add rice noodles, season with the soy sauce mixture, white pepper and chilli sauce, if using, and stir-fry until noodles are charred and well coated in the sauce.

Push the rice noodles to one side to make a clear space in the wok, then add lard crisps and crack the egg into the resulting oil. Breaking up the egg, stir to cover it with noodles and let it cook for 10–15 seconds before you start stir-frying again. Lastly, add bean sprouts and garlic chives, turn the heat off, give everything in the wok a toss to combine, and then tip out onto a serving plate. Serve immediately.

TIP

Fish cake is available ready-made from most Asian grocery stores. It is a traditional ingredient in Chinese cooking, made by blending fish meat into a paste before being steamed. Make lard crisps by rendering small pieces of pork back fat, frying gently until crisp – you can leave them out, but they make a lot of difference to the taste.

BEEF RENDANG
COCONUT BRAISED BEEF

SERVINGS: 6 | PREP TIME: 20 MINS | COOK TIME: 1¼ MINS | SKILL LEVEL: 1 (EASY)

INGREDIENTS

1 kg beef rump, cut into 3 cm cubes
1.5 litres coconut milk
3 tbsp freshly grated coconut
200 g sliced shallots
1 tsp freshly ground mace
100 ml cooking oil
4 cloves sliced garlic
1 stick cinnamon bark
1 stalk bruised lemongrass
2 kaffir lime leaves
1 sheet turmeric leaf
  (available dried or frozen
  in Asian supermarkets)
1 tbsp palm sugar
200 g toasted desiccated coconut

Blended mixture
2½ cm piece of turmeric root
100 g purple shallots
3 cloves
125 g dried ground chilli,
  mixed with a little water
  to form a paste
2½ cm piece of galangal
2½ cm piece of ginger
½ tsp ground black pepper
5 candlenuts

Ground mixture
1 tbsp cumin seeds
1 tsp fennel seeds
5 cloves
1 tbsp coriander seeds

METHOD

Mix beef with 500 ml coconut milk, the grated coconut, 100 g of sliced shallots and the mace. Set aside to marinate for 20–30 minutes.

In a wok, heat cooking oil over a medium heat, then add remaining shallots with garlic and the cinnamon stick, and fry shallots until lightly golden – almost to crispy.

Place all ingredients for blended mixture in a blender and pulse until a smooth paste is formed. Grind spices for ground mixture in a coffee grinder or spice grinder, or a mortar and pestle, to create a fine powder.

Add blended mixture to wok, along with lemongrass, kaffir lime leaves, turmeric leaf, palm sugar, ground mixture and 500 ml coconut milk. Cook over a medium heat until oil starts to visibly separate from the mixture. This should take 2–3 minutes.

Add marinated beef and stir in. Add remaining coconut milk and cook over a medium heat for 50–60 minutes, until there is almost no liquid in the wok and beef is tender. Add desiccated coconut and stir-fry for 3–4 minutes, until dish is dry.

I serve this with yellow glutinous rice.

Aussies love anything that's crumbed and fried, so we wanted to honour the institution that is the humble schnitzel, a favourite in our family. Another hit in our house is Buttermilk pancakes, a weekend indulgence and a tip of the cap to Bill's, a Sydney treasure and a much loved haunt in past times.

Sam & Leah.

SIMONN HAWKE & LEAH MORPHETT
LOLLI REDINI

PORK SCHNITZEL WITH POTATO
RÖSTI,FENNEL SLAW & ROASTED
GARLIC AÏOLI

BUTTERMILK & RICOTTA PANCAKES WITH
HONEYCOMB CREAM, CARAMELISED
BANANAS & MACADAMIAS

ORANGE,
NSW

PORK SCHNITZEL WITH POTATO RÖSTI, FENNEL SLAW & ROASTED GARLIC AÏOLI

SERVINGS: 4 | PREP TIME: 50 MINS | COOK TIME: 30 MINS | SKILL LEVEL: 2 (MODERATE)

INGREDIENTS

Pork schnitzel
1 large pork fillet
½ loaf stale bread –
    ciabatta or
    sourdough batard
1 egg
1 cup milk
1 cup plain flour
salt and pepper
butter for cooking
1 bunch sage leaves, picked

Roasted garlic aïoli
2 heads garlic (or more
    if you like it super-rich)
5 egg yolks, at room
    temperature
120 ml good-quality
    white wine vinegar
2 tsp sea salt
½ tsp ground black pepper
1 tbsp Dijon mustard
300 ml vegetable oil
200 ml olive oil
100 ml warm water

Fennel slaw
¼ cup caster sugar
¼ cup apple cider vinegar
1 sweet fresh carrot
1 bunch fresh mint
1 large super-good
    Granny Smith apple
1 head fennel
¼ small red cabbage
¼ small Savoy cabbage
½ Spanish onion
1 clove garlic, crushed
1 quantity roasted
    garlic aïoli
salt and pepper

Rösti
8 large Désirée potatoes
150 g melted butter
olive oil and extra butter
    for cooking

METHOD

Pork schnitzel: trim the pork and cut into 8 even-sized medallions, then bash out into thin pieces between sheets of plastic wrap.

Make breadcrumbs by whizzing your favourite stale bread in the food processor, and place in a shallow bowl. Mix the egg with the milk to make an egg wash, and place in another shallow bowl. Season the flour and place in a third shallow bowl.

Crumb the pork by first dusting each piece separately in seasoned flour, then dipping in the egg wash, and finally coating in the breadcrumbs. Set aside on a plate in the fridge for cooking later.

When you're ready to cook, melt a decent knob of butter over a medium heat in a frying pan until sizzling. Throw in the sage leaves. Lay the crumbed pork in the sizzling butter and sage. Allow to cook until golden and crispy, then turn over and repeat. It should take about 2–3 minutes on each side.

Depending on how big your pan is you may need to do a couple of batches; keep the first lot warm in the oven at 150°C.

Roasted garlic aïoli: pre-heat the oven to 160°C. Wrap the garlic heads in tinfoil and roast for 40 minutes. Set aside, and when cool enough peel the softened garlic and discard the scraps.

Place the egg yolks, garlic, vinegar, salt, pepper and mustard in a blender and thoroughly combine until smooth. Turn the blender speed down to medium.

Slowly trickle the oils into the blender while it is running. When it becomes too thick, add a little of the warm water. Continue until all the oil is incorporated, then adjust the seasoning to your liking.

The trick is to have all the ingredients at the same temperature and not to run the blender too fast when mixing.

To make the slaw: put the caster sugar in the vinegar to dissolve. Peel and grate the carrot and pick and roughly tear the mint. Shred the apple, fennel, cabbage and onion finely on a Japanese mandolin, or slice as finely as you can by hand. Toss all together and add the sweetened vinegar and crushed garlic.

Add as much aïoli to the salad as you like (I use about half), then adjust the seasoning. Set aside in the fridge.

For the rösti: turn the oven up to 200°C. Grate the potato on the coarse side of a hand grater. Squeeze all of the water out of the potato with your hands, over a sieve or colander, keeping the liquid that results.

Allow the liquid to settle for 10 minutes, until the water separates from the starch (the white stuff that sinks to the bottom of the liquid). Gently tip the water off the top (and discard it), then mix the melted butter and starch through the potato. Season to taste with salt and freshly ground black pepper.

Gently press the grated potato evenly and firmly into a heated, non-stick ovenproof pan that has a little olive oil and butter melted in it, then put in the hot oven. Remove from the oven after about 15 minutes, and flip it over if it is golden-brown and crispy. Put it back in the oven for a further 15 minutes. Cool a little, then cut into wedges when ready to serve.

BUTTERMILK & RICOTTA PANCAKES WITH HONEYCOMB CREAM, CARAMELISED BANANAS & MACADAMIAS

SERVINGS: 6 | PREP TIME: 45 MINS PLUS RESTING
COOK TIME: 5–6 MINS PER PANCAKE | SKILL LEVEL: 2 (MODERATE)

INGREDIENTS

Honeycomb cream

200 g caster sugar

5 tbsp golden syrup

2 tsp bicarbonate of soda

2 cups 45% fat cream
   (or ordinary cream if
   you can't find it)

2 tbsp icing sugar

scraped seeds
   of 1 vanilla bean

Pancakes

3 cups self-raising flour

½ tsp bicarbonate of soda

3 tbsp icing sugar

pinch of salt

2 eggs

150 g melted butter

1 cup buttermilk

1 cup ordinary milk

250 g ricotta

butter for cooking

*Caramelised bananas
and macadamias*

50 g butter to cook
   bananas in

4 nice bananas,
   cut in half lengthways
   or into fat chunks

1 cup toasted and roughly
   chopped macadamias

½ cup brandy (optional...
   for effect to impress
   the kids!)

1½ cups brown sugar

1½ cups single
   pouring cream

150 g unsalted butter,
   diced and chilled

METHOD

Honeycomb cream: grease a 20 cm square tin, or any tin tray, with butter or a non-stick spray. Mix the sugar and golden syrup in a deep saucepan and stir over a gentle heat until the sugar dissolves. Turn up the heat and simmer until you have an amber caramel colour. Quickly take away from the heat and beat in the bicarbonate of soda with a wooden spoon until absorbed and the caramel is foaming. Scrape the mix onto the tin or tray. Allow to cool for about an hour. Break up and store in a cool, dry place in an airtight container.

When ready to do the pancakes, roughly crush enough honeycomb to give 1 cupful. Whip the cream, add the icing sugar and vanilla seeds, then fold in the crushed honeycomb. Put in a bowl in the fridge while you cook the pancakes.

Pancake mix: sift the dry ingredients into a bowl. Make a well in the centre and add the eggs. Gradually whisk in the two milks. Incorporate the melted butter, and whisk until nice and smooth. Fold the ricotta in at the last minute. Cover and rest in the fridge for an hour minimum... best overnight.

Caramelised bananas and macadamias: melt the 50 g of butter in a large non-stick frying pan and bring to a gentle sizzle. Add the bananas and cook until nice and golden on each side. Take the bananas out and set aside.

Add the toasted macadamias to the pan. Flambé with the brandy (if wished) – watch out for the eyebrows! Add the brown sugar and cream, boil until smooth and then whisk in the cold butter.

Return the bananas to the pan and set aside... time to make the pancakes!

Pancakes: pre-heat the oven to 100°C to keep the pancakes warm as you cook them. Melt a bit of butter in a pan, and bring to a medium heat until gently sizzling. Dollop your pancake mix into the pan, as big or small as you like.

The pancakes will be ready to turn after they have risen and have bubbles forming on the top – don't turn until you see this, or they will be stodgy in the middle. They need about 2–3 minutes each side.

Keep repeating the process, wiping the pan out in between pancakes. Store the cooked pancakes on a plate in the oven until you're ready to serve, or just dish them out to the happy campers as you go – you will have to wait for yours!

To serve: top pancakes with the warm caramelised banana mix and dollop a big spoonful of honeycomb cream on top. Garnish with extra honeycomb and add more things if you like, e.g. bacon, strawberries, maple syrup...

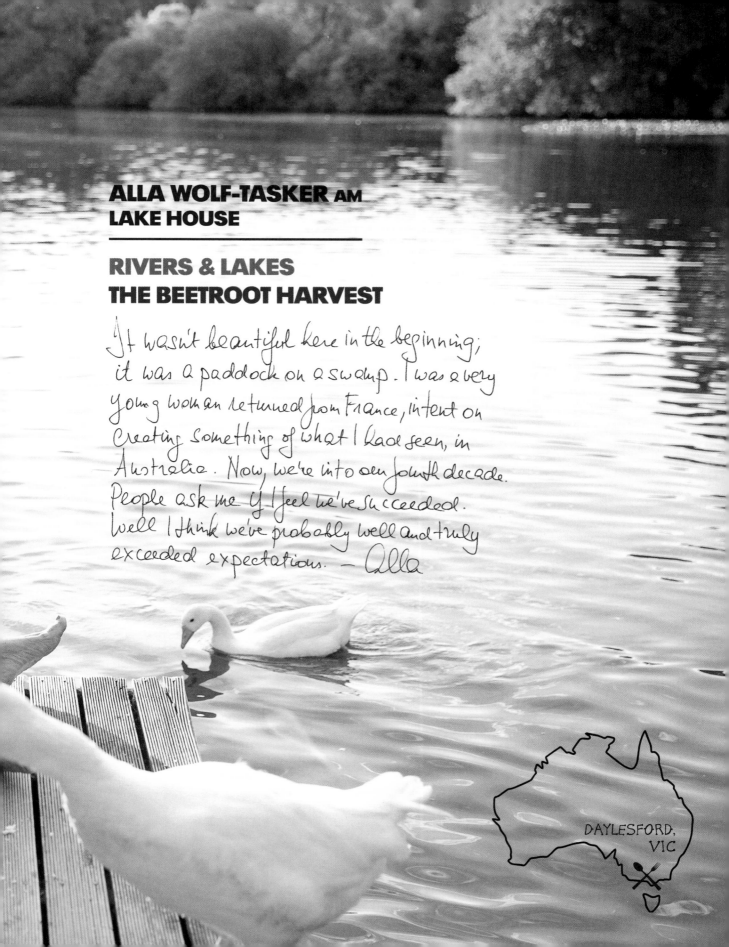

ALLA WOLF-TASKER AM
LAKE HOUSE

RIVERS & LAKES
THE BEETROOT HARVEST

It wasn't beautiful here in the beginning;
it was a paddock on a swamp. I was a very
young woman returned from France, intent on
creating something of what I had seen, in
Australia. Now, we're into our fourth decade.
People ask me if I feel we've succeeded.
Well I think we've probably well and truly
exceeded expectations. — Alla

DAYLESFORD,
VIC

RIVERS & LAKES
A SHARED PLATTER

SERVINGS: 2–3 | PREP TIME: 2 HOURS PLUS CURING | SKILL LEVEL: 3 (CHALLENGING)

This dish is made up of several recipes. They are wonderful combined and beautiful on their own, and great added to something else in your own way.

INGREDIENTS

Cure mix
600 g salt
400 g sugar
zest of 2 lemons
12 fennel fronds,
  finely chopped

1 fillet from a 2 kg
  Murray cod, cleaned
  and skinned
  (reserve bones)
1 x 300–400 g
  freshwater trout
  pin-boned and skinned
  (reserve skin and bones)
1 medium-sized smoked
  eel, filleted (reserve
  skin, head and bones)
2 small yabbies
  (or 1 large) per person,
  shelled (reserve shells)
40–60 ml extra
  virgin olive oil
2–3 sprigs thyme
2–3 strips lemon zest

Watercress purée
1 bunch watercress
zest and juice of 1 lemon
extra virgin olive oil

Mustard crème fraîche
250 ml crème fraîche
6–8 drops mustard oil

To finish
1 tsp lilliput (tiny) capers,
  rinsed and drained
zest of 1 lemon
4 tsp finely diced
  cucumber
oil for deep-frying
wild fennel fronds
  and flowers
watercress

METHOD

To cure the fish: mix all cure mix ingredients evenly together. To cure the Murray cod, spread a quarter of the cure mix over a square of plastic wrap. Place fillet on top, cover with another quarter of the cure mix and wrap up tightly in the plastic. Refrigerate for 2 hours. To cure the trout, use remaining cure mix to prepare in the same way, but only cure for 30 minutes. Remove both fish from the wrap and wash off the cure. Pat fish dry with paper towel. Refrigerate, covered with plastic wrap, until ready to use.

Trout skin crackling: trim trout skins and scrape clean. Dry out in a gas oven with just the pilot light on or under heat lamps for about 30 minutes. This can also be done in a dehydrator. Once completely dry, store skin in an airtight container until ready to use.

Smoked eel: divide fillets into three equal lengths and stack each of these on top of one another. Press each stack together to form a neat rectangle and wrap tightly with plastic wrap. Freeze into a neat rectangular block. Once frozen, use an electric slicer to shave long, flat slices of frozen smoked eel directly onto small pieces of baking paper, lining up 3–4 slices next to each other (carpaccio style) on each piece of paper. Reserve any trimmings to make smoked fish stock or rillettes. Store the slices on the papers, stacked on top of each other in the fridge.

Yabbies: set a sous vide machine to 52°C. Gut the yabby tails, wash thoroughly and pat dry with paper towel. Place 2 tails at a time into a sous vide bag, together with 20 ml of extra virgin olive oil, 1 sprig of thyme and one strip of lemon zest. Place in the sous vide machine and poach at 52°C for 12 minutes for large yabbies. For the smaller ones, place three in a bag and cook for 8–12 minutes, depending on size. Cool by plunging the bags into iced water. Refrigerate the bags.

Watercress purée: wash watercress thoroughly and blanch for 40 seconds in a pot of boiling water. Drain and shock in iced water. Drain again and pat dry with paper towel. Chop watercress, then purée in a blender with lemon zest and juice and sufficient olive oil to make a paste. Pass through a tamis (drum sieve) and refrigerate.

Mustard crème fraîche: combine crème fraîche and mustard oil. Add a few pinches of salt to make a well-seasoned, lightly pungent accompaniment.

To finish: dice cured trout. Gently mix with lilliput capers, lemon zest and cucumber. Refrigerate until ready to serve. Slice Murray cod on an angle as for sashimi.

Cut each dried trout skin in half with scissors. Heat oil in a deep-fryer to 200°C. Fry each skin piece individually and very quickly – only until the skin expands – using tongs to keep moving the skin through the oil. Drain on paper towel. Season with salt and preferably use immediately.

Assembly: turn a small paper-ful of eel slices onto the middle of a serving platter. Position slices of Murray cod at each end of the eel slices. Intersperse with mounds of cured trout mix and the yabbies. Add quenelles of mustard crème fraîche in the middle or around the eel slices – use these to anchor pieces of trout skin crackling. Place small dollops or quenelles of watercress purée around the assembly. Garnish with fronds and flowers of wild fennel and watercress.

THE BEETROOT HARVEST

SERVINGS: 2–4 | PREP TIME: 1 HOUR | COOK TIME: 30–40 MINS | SKILL LEVEL: 2 (MODERATE)

INGREDIENTS

Baby beetroots

8 baby beetroots
   (may be different colours)
½ cup sugar
1 tbsp red wine vinegar

Beetroot remoulade

2 medium beetroots
150 ml good home-made
   mayonnaise
1 tsp Dijon mustard
2 shallots, diced finely
1 tsp lilliput (tiny) capers,
   washed and drained
1 medium crunchy dill
   cucumber, diced finely

Roast beetroots

1 medium beetroot
olive oil to dress
Chioggia carpaccio
1 medium chioggia beetroot

Garnish

seasonal herbs and
   edible flowers

METHOD

Baby beetroots: wash baby beetroots, leaving 2 cm of stem on. If still intact, scrub but do not trim off the roots. Place all ingredients in a pot along with enough water to cover – if using different coloured beetroots, you will need to cook them separately. Cover with a circle of greaseproof paper, and simmer till cooked; about 15 minutes. Cool beetroots, then cut off stems. Peel beetroots, including the roots.

Beetroot remoulade: pre-heat oven to 165°C. Wrap beetroots in tinfoil and roast for about 30– 40 minutes or until easily pierced with a knife. (Roast your other beetroots – see below –at the same time.) Cool until easy to handle, then peel and julienne. Mix mayonnaise and mustard to make remoulade dressing, then combine all remaining ingredients, including julienned beetroot. Add salt and pepper to taste.

Roast beetroots: scrub beetroots, wrap in tinfoil and roast 165°C until easily pierced with a knife; about 30–40 minutes. Cool, peel and dice. Toss with a little olive oil, salt and freshly ground pepper.

Chioggia carpaccio: scrub and peel raw chioggia beetroot. (Chioggia is an interesting heirloom variety that has 'bull's-eye' markings. You can also use normal beetroot.) Slice beetroots paper-thin, using a mandolin. Dress with a little olive oil, salt and freshly ground pepper.

Assembly: on a rectangular plate, place an arrangement of diced roast beetroots, whole baby beetroots (halve if large) and spoonsful of beetroot remoulade. Intersperse with quarter- and half-slices of raw chioggia. Garnish with herbs and flowers.

RICHARD OUSBY
STOKEHOUSE BRISBANE

CHOP CHOP GARDEN SALAD
STICKY MEAT SOUP

When I moved into this house, the first thing I wanted to do was to plant a veggie garden. When there's nothing in the fridge you can always go out the back, rip a few things out of the ground, toss them together with whatever condiments you have in the cupboard and it's all you really need.

— Richard

STAFFORD, QLD

CHOP CHOP GARDEN SALAD

INGREDIENTS

6 radishes

4 zucchini

1 head fennel, green fronds removed
  to use as garden herbs (see below)

1 head baby cos lettuce

1 bunch chives

3 handfuls garden herbs (shoots, young leaves,
  flowers, etc. – make sure they are edible)

1 handful each basil and mint

50 g grated Parmesan

2 shallots, finely diced

Dressing

100 ml extra virgin olive oil

1 tsp Dijon mustard

35 ml aged red wine vinegar

½ clove garlic, crushed

METHOD

Using a mandolin with small teeth attached (vegetable slicer), slice the radishes, zucchini and fennel.

Wash the lettuce and herbs in ice-cold water, drain and pat dry with paper towel. Finely slice the lettuce.

Place the dressing ingredients in a jar, put the lid on and shake to mix.

Mix all of the salad ingredients together in a large bowl. Pour dressing over as desired, and serve immediately.

STICKY MEAT SOUP
HEARTY BRAISED LAMB SHANKS

INGREDIENTS

2 onions, chopped

2 large carrots

4 sticks celery

2 large leeks,
  green tops removed

3 cloves garlic

50 ml olive oil

5 lamb shanks

100 ml white wine

3 litres chicken stock

2 sprigs thyme

1 bay leaf

handful of parsley

METHOD

Pre-heat the oven to 150°C.

Peel all the vegetables and cut into large (50-cent size) pieces.

Heat olive oil in the bottom of a casserole dish and brown the shanks. This can be done in batches if space in the dish is a problem. After 5 minutes, or when the shanks are golden-brown, remove them from the dish.

In the same dish, sauté the onion, carrot, celery, leek and garlic until the onion goes clear.

Add the shanks back to the pot and deglaze with the white wine, reducing the wine until it is almost gone. Add the chicken stock, thyme, 2 good pinches of salt and the bay leaf. Bring to a simmer. Place in the oven for 2 hours, until the lamb is very soft and falling off the bone.

Season the soup with salt, pepper and parsley. Carefully spoon one shank into each serving bowl, then divide the vegetables and broth evenly among them. Serve with sliced crusty bread smeared with butter.

JOHN EVANS & SONIA GREIG
SOUTH ON ALBANY

POTATO & LEEK SOUP WITH MUSSELS & WELSH LAVERBREAD
BRAISED BEEF CHEEKS WITH CARROT PURÉE & HERB BRIOCHE CRUMBS

Growing up in Wales, my family would cook up a lot of soups, stews and slow braises. Looking back, it was probably so that they could go to the pub — but that's the beauty of slow cooking. You can put it on, go out and have fun, and come back and dinner's done.

John

BERRY, NSW

POTATO & LEEK SOUP WITH MUSSELS & WELSH LAVERBREAD

SERVINGS: 4 | PREP TIME: 1 HOUR PLUS DRYING | COOK TIME: 50 MINS | SKILL LEVEL: 1 (EASY)

INGREDIENTS

750 ml vegetable
or chicken stock

700 g trimmed and
washed leek,
white part only

110 g unsalted butter,
chopped

350 g peeled and
diced potatoes

100 ml cream

16 mussels, scrubbed
and beards removed

¼ cup white wine

1 shallot, finely sliced

3 sprigs thyme

extra virgin olive oil,
to serve

2 tsp finely chopped
chives, to serve

Dried Welsh laverbread

1 x 120 g can Welsh
laverbread (or use
store-bought sheets
of dried nori)

METHOD

To dry the laverbread, line two baking sheets with baking paper. Spread the laverbread out thinly over the paper and leave in a warm place for 4–5 hours (sitting on top of a hot oven works well), until dried out. Set aside to cool to room temperature, then tear into small pieces and store in an airtight container. (If using nori sheets, tear into small pieces.)

To make the soup, bring the stock to the boil in a saucepan.

In a separate saucepan, sweat the leek and 60 g of butter with a good pinch of sea salt over a low heat for 5 minutes, stirring occasionally, until softened. Add the boiling stock and the potatoes, and simmer for 30 minutes or until the potatoes are well cooked.

Add the cream and remaining butter, some salt and white pepper and blend in batches until smooth. Pass through a fine sieve and return to a clean saucepan. Check for seasoning and consistency, adding a little water if needed, and keep warm.

To cook the mussels, heat a medium saucepan over a high heat, then add the mussels, white wine, shallot and thyme. Cover with a tight-fitting lid. After 1 minute, check the mussels and give the pan a good shake, then replace the lid and cook for 1 more minute. Repeat until all the mussels are open, then drain immediately. (Discard any mussels that will not open after a few minutes.)

Place the mussels in warmed bowls and ladle the soup over. Drizzle some olive oil on top and serve sprinkled with some chives and a few shards of dried laverbread.

TIP

Laverbread is a natural seaweed from Wales. A much-loved delicacy, it is often served as part of a traditional Welsh breakfast with bacon, eggs and cockles.

BRAISED BEEF CHEEKS WITH CARROT PURÉE & HERB BRIOCHE CRUMBS

SERVINGS: 6 | PREP TIME: 40 MINS PLUS MARINATING
COOK TIME: 3½–4 HOURS | SKILL LEVEL: 1 (EASY)

INGREDIENTS

6 untrimmed beef cheeks
 (2 kg; or 1.3 kg trimmed)

2½ cups full-bodied
 red wine

6 cloves garlic, peeled
 and crushed with
 the back of a knife

12 sprigs thyme

1 orange, quartered

10 black peppercorns

6 juniper berries

1½ tbsp vegetable oil

200 g pancetta or
 thick bacon, chopped
 into lardons

2 large brown onions,
 cut into wedges

2.5 litres beef stock

1½ tbsp tomato paste

3 carrots, cut in half

Carrot purée

1 kg carrots, peeled
 and chopped

2 star anise

1 tbsp olive oil

500 ml freshly
 squeezed orange juice

Herb brioche crumbs

½ loaf brioche
 (approx. 150 g)

½ bunch flat-leaf parsley,
 leaves picked to yield
 20 g, then chopped

To serve

steamed green beans

METHOD

If necessary, trim beef cheeks of any fat and sinew. Place cheeks in a non-reactive (stainless-steel, glass or enamel) container with red wine, garlic, thyme, orange quarters, peppercorns and juniper berries. Mix to combine, cover and refrigerate overnight.

Pre-heat oven to 160°C.

Drain beef cheeks in a colander, reserving the marinade. Pat cheeks dry with paper towel and season with salt and pepper. Pre-heat a heavy casserole dish over a medium-high heat. Add half the oil and brown half of the beef cheeks for 1–2 minutes each side or until well browned. Remove and set aside. Add remaining oil and brown remaining beef cheeks. Set aside.

Add pancetta or bacon to the pan with onion and cook for 3 minutes, stirring occasionally, until golden. Strain the wine from the other marinade ingredients, add to the pan and boil for 1 minute, add beef stock, tomato paste, beef cheeks and any juices, and stir to combine. Add remaining marinade ingredients and carrots, cover and cook in the oven for 3½ hours. Check the cheeks to see if they are tender – cook for a further 30 minutes if needed.

Meanwhile, make the carrot purée. Place carrot, star anise and oil in a medium saucepan over a medium-low heat and sweat for 10–15 minutes, stirring occasionally, without colouring. Add the orange juice, cook until really soft, and then strain, reserving the cooking liquid and discarding the star anise. Transfer carrots to a high-speed blender and gradually add enough of the reserved liquid to help blend to a nice smooth purée. Season to taste.

Meanwhile, to make the herb brioche crumbs, trim and discard the crusts from the brioche to yield 100 g. Cut into pieces and add to the bowl of a food processor with the parsley and pulse to form fine crumbs.

Remove beef cheeks from the oven, remove and discard the orange quarters and any thyme stems, and, using a slotted spoon, carefully transfer beef, carrot, onion and everything else to a warmed serving dish. Cover and set aside.

Place casserole dish over a medium heat and bring cooking liquor to the boil. Simmer rapidly for 8 minutes or until reduced to about 400 ml, then pour over the beef cheeks and serve with carrot purée and steamed beans, with herb brioche crumb sprinkled over the beef cheeks.

MICHAEL KLAUSEN
BRASSERIE BREAD

THE BEST FRENCH
TOAST EVER!
CHOCOLATE MOUSSE
WITH RASPBERRY COULIS &
DARK SALTED CARAMEL

NORTH BONDI,
NSW

I've become known as 'Mr Bread man' and 'Brasserie Bread Guy' and 'the Bread Guy'. I am happy with that. I love that I work with flour, water and salt, and nothing else, and I can create so many different things by using time and fermentation and different temperatures. Understanding how soil develops flavour in a grain, which develops the flavour in the bread.

— Michael

THE BEST FRENCH TOAST EVER!

SERVINGS: 4 | PREP TIME: 10 MINS PLUS SOAKING | COOK TIME: 20 MINS | SKILL LEVEL: 1 (EASY)

INGREDIENTS

4 slices real sourdough
bread, cut 2 cm thick

4 eggs

1¼ cups milk

1 tsp finely
grated orange rind

½ tsp vanilla paste

pinch of salt

2 punnets fresh
strawberries

juice of 1 orange

2 tbsp caster sugar

butter for cooking
the French toast

METHOD

Place bread in a single layer in a shallow dish (the bread should fit snugly in the dish).

Crack eggs into a bowl and add milk, orange rind, vanilla and salt. Whisk to combine. (I call this the 'custard' for the French toast). Pour the custard over the bread. Refrigerate for at least 1 hour, preferably overnight. Turn occasionally. It is important that all the bread soaks up the custard.

Lightly stew strawberries with orange juice and sugar for 2–3 minutes and set aside.

Heat butter in a large frying pan over a medium heat until just starting to brown. Add bread and reduce temperature to low. Cook for about 8–10 minutes each side, or until golden-brown.

Serve immediately with strawberries, and their orange and sugar syrup.

CHOCOLATE MOUSSE WITH RASPBERRY COULIS & DARK SALTED CARAMEL

SERVINGS: 4 | PREP TIME: 45 MINS | SKILL LEVEL: 2 (MODERATE)

INGREDIENTS

Chocolate mousse

110 g good-quality chocolate (64% or darker)

2 organic egg yolks

2 tbsp vanilla syrup (you can buy vanilla syrup from coffee industry suppliers, I use Heilala vanilla syrup)

3 organic egg whites

20 g sugar

240 ml cream

Raspberry coulis

1 tbsp sugar

2 tbsp water

100 g fresh or frozen and thawed raspberries

Salted caramel (makes 260 ml)

225 g caster sugar

150 ml water

70 ml double cream, warmed

80 g butter, coarsely chopped

2 g (a little less than ½ tsp) sea salt

METHOD

Chocolate mousse: melt chocolate in a bowl.

Whisk egg yolks and vanilla syrup in a bain marie or in a heatproof bowl set over a pan of simmering water until ribbon stage – if you allow some mixture to fall from the spoon, it will slowly form a ribbon on the surface that will hold its shape for a short while.

Whisk egg whites to soft peaks, then add sugar and whisk to stiff peaks.

Whip the cream to soft peaks.

Add melted chocolate to the yolk mixture, then fold in the egg white, keeping the mixture airy. Gently fold in the whipped cream. Place in a bowl and refrigerate overnight.

Raspberry coulis: heat the sugar and water in a small saucepan over a medium heat, stirring from time to time, until the sugar dissolves completely.

Put the raspberries and the sugar syrup in a blender and purée. If you would like a very smooth finish, strain it through a fine-meshed sieve to remove the seeds. The sauce keeps well, tightly covered, in the fridge for 4–5 days and freezes perfectly for several months.

Salted caramel: combine sugar and water in a heavy-based saucepan and stir over a low heat until sugar dissolves. Increase the heat to high and cook, brushing down sides of pan with a wet pastry brush, until the mixture caramelises to a deep golden colour. Cook it a little longer to get a darker and stronger flavour.

Remove from the heat, add warmed cream, butter and sea salt, and stir to combine (be careful, as mixture will split). Pour into a stainless-steel bowl immediately, to prevent further cooking. You can then transfer to a glass jar for longer storing.

To assemble: in a small glass for each person, layer the mousse with the coulis, some caramel, and even some melted chocolate. Add 1 tablespoon of coulis to the glass, then a small quenelle of mousse, drizzle over some caramel and then 1 teaspoon of melted chocolate. Depending on the serving size, repeat.

I love the ease and simplicity of
roasting a chicken with a few
vegetables and herbs in season.
It's a dish my dad used to cook
a lot when I was growing up.
It really is just a matter of 'throw
it together in one pan, open a
bottle of wine and wait.'

—Dan.

BIRREGURRA,
VIC

SUMMER ROAST CHICKEN

SERVINGS: 4 – OR 2 HUNGRY ADULTS AND A 4-YEAR-OLD | PREP TIME: 20 MINS
COOK TIME: 45 MINS | SKILL LEVEL: 1 (EASY)

INGREDIENTS

Chicken

1 x 1.6 kg organic chicken

handful of tarragon, thyme, fennel tops, lovage (mixed)

1 lemon, cut in half

1 head garlic, cut in half

olive oil to coat

good amount of good salt – Murray River or Pink Lake

Vegetables

2–4 small zucchini, with flowers intact

2–6 small tomatoes per person

as many potatoes as you feel like (such as Bintje, Kipfler or small Dutch Creams)

handful of chopped chives

METHOD

For the chicken: take the chicken from the fridge and out of any plastic packaging about 20–30 minutes before you want to cook it. Pre-heat the oven to 220°C.

Dislocate the chicken legs at the thigh muscle, laying the legs flat but still attached, and remove the wishbone. (This shortens the usual cooking time.)

Stuff herbs, lemon halves and garlic into the cavity and smother the skin with olive oil. Sprinkle a good amount of salt over the skin, and rub the oil and salt into it. Place the chicken on a roasting tray.

For the veg: harvest the veg fresh if possible – all are best just picked. Wash the veg and cut them simply, leaving some of the zucchini flowers whole and splitting the larger ones. Quarter the bigger tomatoes and leave the small ones whole. Peel and cut the potatoes into quarters, or lengthways if using Kipflers.

Arrange the zucchini and tomato around the chicken. Dress everything well with olive oil, season with salt, and place the tray on the bottom rack of the oven.

With the potatoes, it's best to roast them separately and unseasoned so that they crisp up well. Place them in a separate baking dish, cover well with olive oil and place the tray on the top shelf of the oven.

If all goes to plan, everything will be ready in 45 minutes. I leave the oven at 220°C the whole time, then open the door with the oven turned off for 10 minutes once everything is cooked so that the juices distribute nicely through the chicken. Season the zucchini and tomatoes with chives, season the potatoes to taste, carve the chook and serve.

NICK HOLLOWAY
NU NU

**WOOD-ROASTED REEF FISH
WITH PINEAPPLE CURRY**

PALM HEART, PAPAYA,
YOUNG COCONUT
& LYCHEE SALAD

PALM COVE, QLD

WOOD-ROASTED REEF FISH WITH PINEAPPLE CURRY

SERVINGS: 4 | PREP TIME: 2 HOURS | COOK TIME: 1 HOUR | SKILL LEVEL: 2 (MODERATE)

INGREDIENTS

Pineapple curry

5 large dried long red chillies, de-seeded and soaked in water for at least 1 hour, preferably overnight

4 tbsp roughly chopped garlic

5 tbsp roughly chopped red shallots

4 tbsp finely sliced lemongrass, tender inner part only

1 tbsp peeled and grated galangal

1 tbsp washed and scraped coriander roots

1 tbsp fresh turmeric

1 tsp good-quality Thai shrimp paste, roasted (see tip below)

3 tbsp coconut cream

1 tbsp ginger oil (see tip below)

2 kaffir lime leaves, bruised

1–2 tbsp pale palm sugar, crushed

1 cup fish stock

1 tbsp fish sauce (approx.) (start with 1 tsp and add more to taste)

½ pineapple, grated and juice collected

1 tbsp thick tamarind water (see tip below)

juice of 2 limes

Fish

1 beautiful reef fish, 1.2–1.5 kg (I like mine freshly line-caught and brain-spiked)

1 tbsp cane sugar

2 tbsp good-quality fish sauce

3 cups assorted coriander, Thai basil, Vietnamese mint and mint leaves

4 tsp fried garlic crisps

4 tbsp fried shallot crisps

2 kaffir lime leaves, finely sliced into threads

2 lemon leaves, finely sliced into threads

2 limes, sliced into thin rings

handful shaved coconut, toasted in a dry pan

METHOD

First make the pineapple curry. Grind the chilli, garlic, shallots, lemongrass, galangal, coriander roots, turmeric and shrimp paste with a pinch of salt in a food processor or mortar and pestle until very smooth and fine.

Crack coconut cream by simmering it in a heavy-based pot or wok until it splits into a curdled-looking substance. Add ginger oil then add the curry paste with the bruised kaffir lime leaves and fry over an even heat until heady and fragrant. It should take 10–15 minutes and smell beautifully perfumed.

Add the palm sugar and continue to fry for a few moments to caramelise the sugar and deepen the colour. Finally add the stock, fish sauce, grated pineapple and juice, and tamarind water, and bring the curry back to a gentle simmer for another 10 minutes to allow the flavours to coalesce.

Squeeze in the fresh lime juice and adjust the seasoning as necessary. The curry should taste rich, sour and slightly sweet and have a wonderful orange film of oil on top.

Remove and discard the scales, gills and guts from the fish. Score the fish with a sharp knife and then rub it with the sugar and fish sauce. Tuck the seasoned fish into a snug tray and allow it to marinate for 5–10 minutes.

Light a fire using your favourite wood and allow it to burn down to coals. Cook the fish in amongst the coals until it starts to colour, then pour over the prepared curry and simmer until the fish falls from the bone gracefully.

Scatter over the herbs, garlic and shallot crisps, leaf threads, sliced limes and toasted coconut and serve in the tray, alongside the Palm Heart, Papaya, Young Coconut and Lychee Salad.

TIPS

To roast shrimp paste, spread the required quantity onto a double thickness of tinfoil and fold into a flat 'envelope' encasing the paste. Place the packet directly onto the coals or grill of a barbecue and roast for a few minutes each side. Cool.

For ginger oil, place several slices of fresh ginger in 100 ml vegetable oil and warm gently (to 50–60°C). The oil can be used straight away, but will mature further with time if you store it with the ginger left in.

Make tamarind water by breaking up tamarind pulp with your fingers in a little warm water and straining out the seeds.

PALM HEART, PAPAYA, YOUNG COCONUT & LYCHEE SALAD

SERVINGS: 4 | PREP TIME: 20 MINS | SKILL LEVEL: 1 (EASY)

INGREDIENTS

4 cups shaved fresh palm hearts
  (use a peeler)

1 cup shaved honeydew melon

1 cup shaved rock melon

1 cup shredded green papaya

1 cup teenage coconut,
  sliced into strips

12 lychees, peeled and de-seeded

1 cup mint leaves

1 cup hibiscus petals

1 cup finely sliced banana blossom
  (the flower of the banana plant, optional)

½ tsp finely sliced red chilli

2 tsp cane sugar

1 tsp good-quality fish sauce

juice of 2 limes

METHOD

Shave, shred and slice all the ingredients shortly before serving.

Assemble the palm heart, melon, papaya, young coconut, lychees, mint, hibiscus petals, optional banana blossom and chilli in a bowl and dress with the sugar, fish sauce and lime juice. Jumble the salad onto a serving plate and eat immediately with Wood-Roasted Reef Fish with Pineapple Curry.

The complete dish is best served with ice-cold beer or tall icy tropical cocktails.

It feels like food has been an important part of my life for as long as I can remember. While most kids were in the backyard sandpit, I was more often than not on the floor of my parents' fish and chip shop, being pulled away to lend a hand. Work ethic and love of food was never in doubt.

Mano

SOUTH PERTH, WA

PETER MANIFIS
INCONTRO

MEZZE PLATTER FAVOURITES
AVGOLEMONO

MEZZE PLATTER FAVOURITES

SERVINGS: 6–10 | PREP TIME: 45 MINS | COOK TIME: 1 HOUR | SKILL LEVEL: 2 (MODERATE)

INGREDIENTS

Mini spanakopita

Filling

1 bunch spring onions, finely chopped
50 g butter
50 ml olive oil
1 bunch silverbeet, washed and chopped
100 g great-quality feta
  (I like Over The Moon)
50 g Kefalograviera (or haloumi
  if you can't find any), grated
5 eggs, lightly beaten

To finish

8 sheets brik pastry
1 egg, beaten
5 litres canola oil

Keftedes

300 g veal mince
1 cup mint, finely chopped
1 cup flat-leaf parsley, finely chopped
1 large brown onion, grated
4 large ripe tomatoes, grated
up to 1 cup water
up to 1 cup self-raising flour
400 ml canola oil,
  for shallow-frying

Taramasalata

300 g stale white bread, crusts removed
1 x 100 g can white tarama
  (salted, cured cod roe,
  available from most good delis)
¼ brown onion, roughly chopped
1 clove garlic, minced
juice of 2 lemons
¼ cup canola oil
⅓ cup olive oil
ground white pepper to taste
1 cup water

To serve

3 small Lebanese cucumbers
6 pieces of fresh pita bread
200 g Kalamata olives
handful of small, ripe tomatoes
good-quality olive oil
a good few dollops of Greek yoghurt

METHOD

For the mini spanakopita: in a large saucepan on a medium heat, lightly sauté the spring onion in the butter and olive oil until soft. Add in the silverbeet and cover the pan with a lid. Once the mixture has reduced by half, remove the pan from the heat, add the cheeses, eggs and freshly ground pepper to taste. Give everything a stir and set aside to cool.

Heat the canola oil to 180°C in a deep-fryer or a heavy-based pot. Take a sheet of brik pastry and place it onto a clean, damp tea towel. Brush the surface with a little beaten egg and then spoon a little of the mixture down the centre of the pastry sheet. Fold in the ends and roll the pastry like a cigar. Set aside on a tray in the freezer, and repeat until all of the pastry has been used. Freeze these filled pastry cigars for around 10 minutes prior to frying. Fry the cigars for about 2 minutes or until golden-brown and drain on paper towel.

For the keftedes: in a large mixing bowl, combine the mince, mint, parsley and grated onion and tomato, along with a good pinch of salt and pepper. Add about half a cup of water to the mix and then a ¼ cup of flour. Mix thoroughly. You can add a little more water or a little more flour depending on the texture of the mix — it should be slightly wet in the hand, but not sloppy. Form small, bite-sized patties and set aside until ready to cook.

To a heavy-based frying pan on a medium to high heat, add some canola oil and fry the patties for 2 minutes each side or until dark brown. Don't be scared of the mix going crispy — this adds a lovely texture to the keftedes.

Best eaten with Greek yoghurt (naturally!), these are fantastic consumed cold the next day.

For the taramasalata: briefly soak the bread in water and gently squeeze out excess liquid. Blitz the tarama, onion, garlic and softened bread in a blender. Add in most of the lemon juice and half of the oil and a good pinch of white pepper. Blitz again on a slow speed. Gradually add the rest of the oil, until smooth. Taste for seasoning, adding lemon or pepper as needed.

To serve, peel the cucumbers, quarter lengthwise and season with salt flakes. Serve the mini spanakopita, keftedes and taramasalata on a big platter with fresh pita bread, olives, halved tomatoes, cucumber and yoghurt. Drizzle the lot with olive oil, salt and ground pepper.

Oh — and don't forget the ouzo!

AVGOLEMONO
GREEK LEMON CHICKEN SOUP

SERVINGS: 10 | PREP TIME: 1 HOUR 35 MINS | COOK TIME: 20 MINS | SKILL LEVEL: 1 (EASY)

INGREDIENTS

1 whole chicken
  (1.2–1.4 kg)
1 large brown onion
1 carrot, peeled
1 stick celery, peeled
5 cups cold water
150 g short-grain rice,
  washed and drained
3 large eggs, at room
  temperature
juice of 2 lemons
olive oil, for drizzling

METHOD

To prepare this traditional Greek soup, thoroughly wash the chicken and place in a really deep pan or large pot. Push the chicken down to the bottom of the pan with your hands, add the onion, carrot and celery, pour in the water (enough to cover the chicken) and season liberally with salt and freshly ground black pepper.

Place on a high heat, put the lid on and bring the water to the boil. Turn the heat down to a simmer and cook the chicken for about 1¼ hours, skimming off the foam regularly. When the meat starts to fall away from the bones, the chicken is done.

Remove the chicken and vegetables from the broth and strain the broth through a mesh sieve, being careful not to burn yourself. Pour the strained broth into a pot, add the rice, season again with salt and pepper and bring the liquid to the boil. Cook until the rice is soft and starting to fall apart (approximately 10 minutes). Remove from the heat to cool.

While the broth is cooling, separate the egg whites, reserving the yolks, and whisk up the egg white to form soft peaks. Lightly beat the yolks and fold into the egg white with the lemon juice. After 5–10 minutes, ladle a spoonful of the soup into the egg mixture to temper it, then slowly stir the soupy egg mixture into the rest of the soup. The eggs will gently cook in the heat of the soup.

Once the chicken is cool enough to handle, pull the meat from the bones and discard the skin. Serve the soup hot, ladled into bowls with the chicken meat on the side, drizzled with olive oil and cracked pepper.

JIM BERARDO
BERARDO'S

NOOSA CAPRESE SALAD
SPANNER CRAB SPAGHETTINI AL OLIO

I chose these dishes because they are what Noosa
and Italian food are all about.
It makes the most of what's fresh and seasonal,
and there is a sense of ease and lightness that lends
itself well to this subtropical peace I call home.
                                                    Jim

NOOSA,
QLD

NOOSA CAPRESE SALAD

SERVINGS: 4 | PREP TIME: 20 MINS | COOK TIME: 15 MINS | SKILL LEVEL: 2 (MODERATE)

INGREDIENTS

320 g mozzarella
  (I use Cedar Street mozzarella)
400 g ripe tomatoes
  (I use local Noosa Reds)
20 basil leaves
200 ml vinaigrette (see below)

Vinaigrette
200 ml good extra
  virgin olive oil (I use Fat Hen
  extra virgin olive oil)
½ clove garlic, minced
80 ml good red wine vinegar
  (I use Líráh oak-aged shiraz vinegar)

METHOD

Combine all vinaigrette ingredients in a mixing bowl and whisk until incorporated. Adjust balance and seasoning with sea salt and pepper.

Slice and arrange mozzarella and tomatoes on a plate. Dress with vinaigrette and garnish with basil leaves.

Serve with good-quality crusty bread.

SPANNER CRAB SPAGHETTINI AL OLIO
SPANNER CRAB WITH SPAGHETTINI & OIL

SERVINGS: 4 | PREP TIME: 10 MINS | SKILL LEVEL: 1 (EASY)

INGREDIENTS

160 g good-quality
  spaghettini
2 cloves garlic, sliced
30 ml good extra virgin
  olive oil (I use Fat Hen
  extra virgin olive oil)
30 g unsalted butter
200 g raw spanner crab
  (I use Fraser Isle
  spanner crab)
sea salt and white pepper
20 g Parmesan, shaved
½ bunch parsley,
  chopped finely

METHOD

Cook pasta in rapidly boiling salted water according to the packet instructions.

While pasta is cooking, sauté garlic gently in a pan with a little olive oil and butter. Once translucent, add crab and season to taste. Fry for 2–3 minutes.

Once pasta is al dente, mix pasta into crab and garlic mixture. Finish with Parmesan, remaining olive oil and butter and the parsley, and adjust seasoning if necessary.

Serve with good-quality crusty bread.

MINH LE
THE FORAGING QUAIL

SPICY VIETNAMESE CHICKEN WINGS
ROASTED RACK OF LAMB

These dishes represent two sides of me: the food my mother cooked for our Vietnamese family and the Australian influence on food I cook for my own family now. That's the multicultural beauty of our country.

Minh.

NEW FARM, QLD

SPICY VIETNAMESE CHICKEN WINGS

SERVINGS: 6 | PREP TIME: 25 MINS PLUS MARINATING OVERNIGHT
COOK TIME: 2–3 HOURS | SKILL LEVEL: 2 (MODERATE)

INGREDIENTS

100 g fresh ginger
5 bird's eye chillies
100 g garlic, peeled
20 g ground black pepper
1 kg chicken wings
50 ml olive oil
1 kg caster sugar
200 ml fish sauce
6 eggs
1 bunch coriander
1 bunch Thai basil
1 bunch Vietnamese mint
1 bunch mint
2 cups jasmine rice

METHOD

Peel ginger and chop into 1 cm pieces. Place ginger, chillies, garlic and pepper in a food processor and blend to a paste. Cut chicken wings into three, along the joints of the bone, and place in a bowl with the paste. Stir to coat the chicken with the paste, and marinate overnight.

Pour olive oil into a deep saucepan along with sugar. Over a high heat, keep stirring until the sugar is starting to brown and caramelise, then quickly add the marinated chicken wings to the pan. Let the caramel coat the chicken wings – you must keep stirring the whole time.

Once chicken is fully coated, deglaze with fish sauce. Turn heat down to low, put a lid on the pan and let it simmer for 2–3 hours. Make sure to stir every 15 minutes.

In another saucepan, boil eggs for 3 minutes, then refresh in ice water. Peel eggs and add them to the chicken wings 30 minutes before the wings finish.

Pick off all the herb leaves and wash. Set aside to eat fresh with the rice. Wash rice three times, place in a rice cooker (or saucepan), add 2 cups of water and cook until done (about 25 minutes in a rice cooker or 20 minutes on the stovetop; I highly recommend the rice cooker).

ROASTED RACK OF LAMB

SERVINGS: 6 | PREP TIME: 30 MINS | COOK TIME: 20 MINS | SKILL LEVEL: 1 (EASY)

INGREDIENTS

2 lamb racks
  (standard 8-rib racks)
oil for cooking

Salad

half a Kent (Japanese)
  pumpkin
1 bunch sage, chopped
100 g pine nuts
500 g green beans
200 g spinach
200 g feta
1 punnet heirloom
  cherry tomatoes
100 g mixed olives,
  stones in

Dressing

200 ml extra virgin olive oil
100 ml balsamic vinegar
30 g sea salt
10 g freshly ground pepper
50 g sugar

(GF)

METHOD

Pre-heat the oven to 200°C.

Season lamb racks with some salt and pepper. Heat a little oil in a 30 cm pan until it starts to smoke. Seal lamb racks – skin-side down first, then seal all the other sides. Place lamb on a roasting tray and put in the oven. Cook for 15 minutes for medium-rare, 5 minutes more for medium, and so on. Rest lamb for 5 minutes.

Peel pumpkin and cut into wedges, seasoning well. Place on oven tray with sage and pine nuts. Place in oven to roast; it should take about 20 minutes.

Bring a pan of water to the boil for the beans. Once water is boiling, cook beans for 3 minutes then place straight into ice water to refresh. Drain well, then cut each into three on an angle.

Now start to make your salad by putting everything into a large salad bowl: beans, spinach, feta, cherry tomatoes cut in half and olives. Add pumpkin once it has cooled a little.

Make a balsamic dressing by whisking extra virgin olive oil and balsamic vinegar with some salt, pepper and sugar, until it comes together. Dress salad when ready to serve.

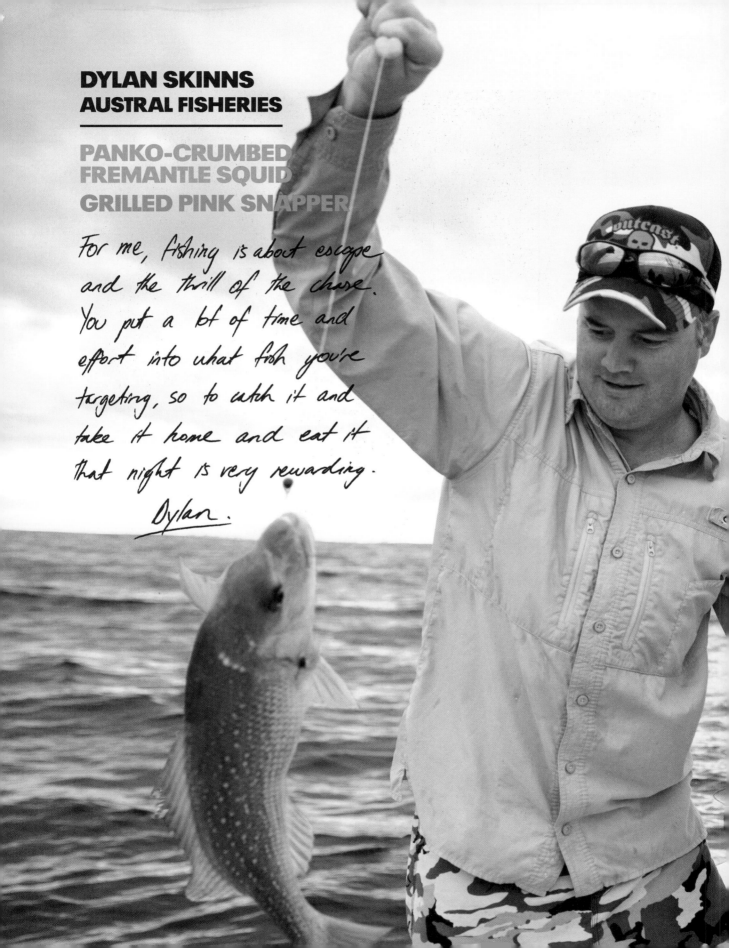

DYLAN SKINNS
AUSTRAL FISHERIES

PANKO-CRUMBED
FREMANTLE SQUID
GRILLED PINK SNAPPER

For me, fishing is about escape
and the thrill of the chase.
You put a lot of time and
effort into what fish you're
targeting, so to catch it and
take it home and eat it
that night is very rewarding.

Dylan.

ROTTNEST ISLAND,
WA

PANKO-CRUMBED FREMANTLE SQUID

SERVINGS: 4 – ENTRÉE SIZE | PREP TIME: 10 MINS | COOK TIME: 2 MINS | SKILL LEVEL: 1 (EASY)

INGREDIENTS

500 g approx. cleaned
  local Fremantle squid
  tubes (2 tubes)
2 eggs
1 x 250 g packet
  Japanese panko crumbs
vegetable oil to fill
  a deep-fryer or
  a shallow-fry wok
1 cup plain flour
4 lemon wedges

METHOD

Cut squid tubes into evenly sized rings, about 1 cm thick.

Prepare egg wash by beating eggs with a little water added and add a sprinkle of sea salt and cracked pepper to the mix. Place panko crumbs in a large open container. Heat oil in a deep-fryer or wok, ready to cook the squid.

Pour flour into a large food-grade zip-lock bag. Add squid rings to bag, and seal with enough air inside to create a good-sized air pocket. Tumble the bag with your hands to ensure all the rings are dusted evenly with flour.

Remove squid from flour and mix through egg wash. Place rings in container of panko crumbs and press crumbs firmly onto each ring to ensure that a good coating is achieved.

Add coated rings to hot oil and cook for 2 minutes or until golden-brown. (If cooking in a wok, cook for 1 minute each side.) Allow cooked rings to rest on paper towel and serve with fresh lemon wedges.

GRILLED PINK SNAPPER

SERVINGS: 2 | PREP TIME: 5 MINS | COOK TIME: 5–6 MINS | SKILL LEVEL: 1 (EASY)

INGREDIENTS

500 g pink snapper fillets
  (1 or 2 fillets), skin and
  bones removed
1 cup plain flour
100 g salted butter
salad of your choice
  to serve
4 lemon wedges

METHOD

With a sharp knife, cut snapper fillets into evenly sized chunks, about 5 cm x 5 cm.

Pour flour into a large food-grade zip-lock bag. Add snapper portions to bag, and seal with enough air inside to create a good-sized air pocket. Tumble the bag with your hands to ensure all fish portions are dusted evenly with flour.

Heat a large non-stick frying pan with butter, and add dusted snapper portions once butter has melted. Cook for 2–3 minutes each side, squeezing a lemon wedge into the melting butter for extra taste.

Remove fish from pan once golden-brown, and allow to rest on paper towel for a few minutes. Serve with your favourite salad or vegetables, along with lemon wedges for an extra flavour dimension. Sprinkle sea salt and cracked pepper over, as desired.

DIANE HOLUIGUE OAM
THE FRENCH KITCHEN

COQ AU VIN
TARTE AUX PIGNONS

I always say, "Make a tart when someone unexpectedly comes to dinner." The pastry takes five minutes and you can throw anything onto it, whether it is a few apples from the bowl or, in this case, succulent glacé fruit.

ARMADALE,
VIC

COQ AU VIN
CHICKEN BRAISED IN RED WINE

SERVINGS: 6 | PREP TIME: 1¼ HOURS | SKILL LEVEL: 1 (EASY)

INGREDIENTS

60 g margarine

1.6 kg chicken,
  cut into 8 pieces,
  plus 2 extra thighs

1 onion, chopped

2 well-rounded tbsp
  plain flour

500 ml red wine

300 ml beef stock

1 bouquet garni

1 beef stock cube

1 heaped tsp tomato paste

3 shallots, finely chopped

1 clove garlic,
  finely chopped

Garnish

12–15 pickling onions
  (or whole shallots)

a little butter

60 g continental bacon
  (speck), cut into bite-sized
  pieces (lardons)

150 g champignons
  (button mushrooms)

1 tsp sugar

2 tbsp chopped parsley

METHOD

In a large casserole or a deep frying pan with a lid, heat the margarine and fry the chicken pieces until well-browned. (Use margarine because butter burns, and oil sits un-absorbed on the top of the sauce.) Add the onion and allow to brown a little also. Sprinkle the flour over, and stir to the bottom of the pan to form a roux (you may need a little extra margarine if the pan is too dry to absorb the flour). Add the liquids, bouquet garni, stock cube, tomato paste, shallots and garlic, and season with salt and freshly milled black pepper. Place the lid on and simmer gently for about 45 minutes, turning the chicken pieces once.

Meanwhile, boil the onions for the garnish in salted water until softened (the time depends on their size), then drain and set aside. When the chicken is cooked, heat some butter in a small frying pan and fry the bacon until crisp and rendered. Add to the chicken. In the rendered bacon fat, plus more butter if necessary, fry the champignons – whole if tiny, or cut into chunky pieces. When fried, add to the casserole. Fry the cooked small onions, adding the sugar to caramelise them a little, then add to the chicken.

To serve, transfer the chicken pieces to a serving platter. Boil down the sauce to a nice sauce consistency. Check the seasoning, and coat the chicken with the sauce and garnish. Sprinkle with the parsley.

TARTE AUX PIGNONS
PINE NUT TART

SERVINGS: 8 | PREP TIME: 30 MINS PLUS MACERATING
COOK TIME: 35–50 MINS | SKILL LEVEL: 2 (MODERATE)

INGREDIENTS

Shortcrust pastry
200 g plain flour
100 g unsalted butter,
  well softened or cut
  into small pieces
3–4 level tbsp caster sugar
1 egg yolk
2–3 tbsp water

Filling
230–300 g chopped glacé
  fruit (focusing on orange,
  orange rinds and citron)
3 tbsp Grand Marnier
grated rind of 1 orange
150 g very soft butter
125 g caster sugar
125 g almond meal
3 eggs
150 g pine nuts

METHOD

The pastry: make the pastry and rest it for 30 minutes minimum (the pastry may be made the day before, when you macerate the fruit). Place the flour on a cool surface. Make a well (hole) in the centre and add the butter, sugar, egg yolk and 1½ tablespoons of water. With your fingers, mix the ingredients in the well, then gradually incorporate the flour, adding the remaining water bit by bit until the dough forms a ball. Alternatively, place the ingredients minus the water in a food processor and pulse together. Then add just enough water (probably less than in the hand-kneaded recipe) to allow the pastry to form into a ball above the blade. Flour a cool surface, and bring together with your hands until light and springy. Form the pastry into a ball, wrap in plastic wrap and rest in the fridge for 10 minutes — no longer, as it's harder to roll when it's too firm.

When ready, roll out the pastry and use it to line a 28 cm tart mould. The pastry should be blind-baked (use blind-baking beans, or ordinary dried beans or rice work just as well) to ensure the base is well cooked through after filling. To do this, prick the pastry, line the base with tinfoil leaving the edges exposed, prick the tart through the tinfoil and bake for 10 minutes at 200°C.

The filling: macerate the glacé fruit by placing in a bowl with the Grand Marnier and orange rind, and leaving in the fridge for a few hours or overnight.

Pre-heat the oven to 190°C. In a bowl or food processor, cream the butter and sugar together until pale and fluffy, then add the almond meal and eggs. Transfer to a bowl and add the glacé fruit. Mix well, then spread over the pastry. Add the pine nuts, pushing them down into the creamed mixture. Bake for approximately 30–35 minutes, depending on desired colour.

Serve cooled to room temperature, but not refrigerated. If desired, dredge with icing sugar.

FIONA WEIR WALMSLEY & ADAM WALMSLEY
BUENA VISTA FARM

MARRY ME CARAMEL BISCUITS
VISITOR BISCUITS
CHICKEN LIVER PÂTÉ

These recipes all come from someone we love who got them from someone they love. The Visitor Biscuits are my Grandma's recipe and they are so quick to make that by the time the kettle is boiled, the bikkies are in the oven. The pâté comes from my friend Jodie who got it from her Uncle Vic. And the caramel biscuits are so delicious you will want to marry them.

Fiona

GERRINGONG, NSW

MARRY ME CARAMEL BISCUITS

MAKES: 20 | PREP TIME: 25 MINS PLUS CHILLING | COOK TIME: 15 MINS | SKILL LEVEL: 1 (EASY)

INGREDIENTS

Shortbread
250 g butter, cold
1 cup rice flour
1½ cups plain flour
1 cup icing sugar
1 egg

Caramel
60 g butter
1 x 395 g can sweetened
   condensed milk
2 tbsp golden syrup

METHOD

Pre-heat the oven to 180°C. Line several baking trays with non-stick baking paper.

The very best way to make this shortbread is in a food processor. Cut the butter into the flours and icing sugar and mix well in a food processor until completely combined and crumbly. Then add the egg and pulse until it forms a firm ball. Wrap in plastic wrap and chill in the fridge for 30 minutes, then roll out to approximately ½ cm thick and use a small round circle cutter to cut out circles. Bake on trays for approximately 15 minutes, or until golden. Transfer to wire racks to cool.

If you don't have a food processor, rub the butter into the flours and sugar with your fingers until combined and crumbly. Make a well in the centre of the mix and add the egg. Keep mixing until smooth and amalgamated and you can form it into a firm ball. Wrap in plastic wrap and proceed as above.

To make the caramel, melt the butter with the condensed milk and golden syrup in a wide, heavy-based saucepan, stirring until golden and bubbling. Keep it at boiling point for at least 5 minutes, stirring continuously, until it thickens and sizzles off the side of the saucepan. Cool slightly, enough to spoon it into a piping bag.

Pipe a dollop of caramel onto the underside of a shortbread round, then press another round on top, creating a sandwich. The caramel will firm as it cools.

VISITOR BISCUITS
CHOCOLATE CHIP BIKKIES

MAKES: 15 | PREP TIME: 10 MINS | COOK TIME: 15 MINS | SKILL LEVEL: 1 (EASY)

INGREDIENTS

125 g butter, softened
1 cup firmly packed
  brown sugar
½ tsp salt
1 tsp pure vanilla extract
1 egg
2 cups self-raising flour
½ cup (or more)
  chocolate pieces

METHOD

Pre-heat the oven to 180°C. Line 1–2 baking trays with non-stick baking paper.

Cream the butter and sugar with salt and vanilla.

Add the egg, then the flour and chocolate pieces.

Ball up into about 15 bikkies and bake for about 15 minutes. Transfer to a wire rack to cool.

CHICKEN LIVER PÂTÉ

SERVINGS: 8 | PREP TIME: 20 MINS | SKILL LEVEL: 1 (EASY)

INGREDIENTS

1 rasher bacon

1 clove garlic

¼ onion

125 g butter

250 g chicken liver,
    washed and
    sinew removed

½ tsp ground nutmeg

handful of basil

2 tbsp Grand Marnier

1 tbsp cream

80 g melted butter,
    to cover

METHOD

Finely chop the bacon, garlic and onion and sauté in the butter in a saucepan or frying pan over a low heat until cooked (approximately 5 minutes).

Add the liver and cook over a low heat until thoroughly cooked (approximately 5 minutes).

Add the nutmeg, pepper to taste, basil, Grand Marnier and cream, and stir everything together. Cook for a further 2 minutes over a low heat then blitz very thoroughly in a food processor or with a hand blender until very, very smooth.

Put into a jar or pot and cover with melted butter. Keeps in the fridge for about a week if you've used very fresh liver.

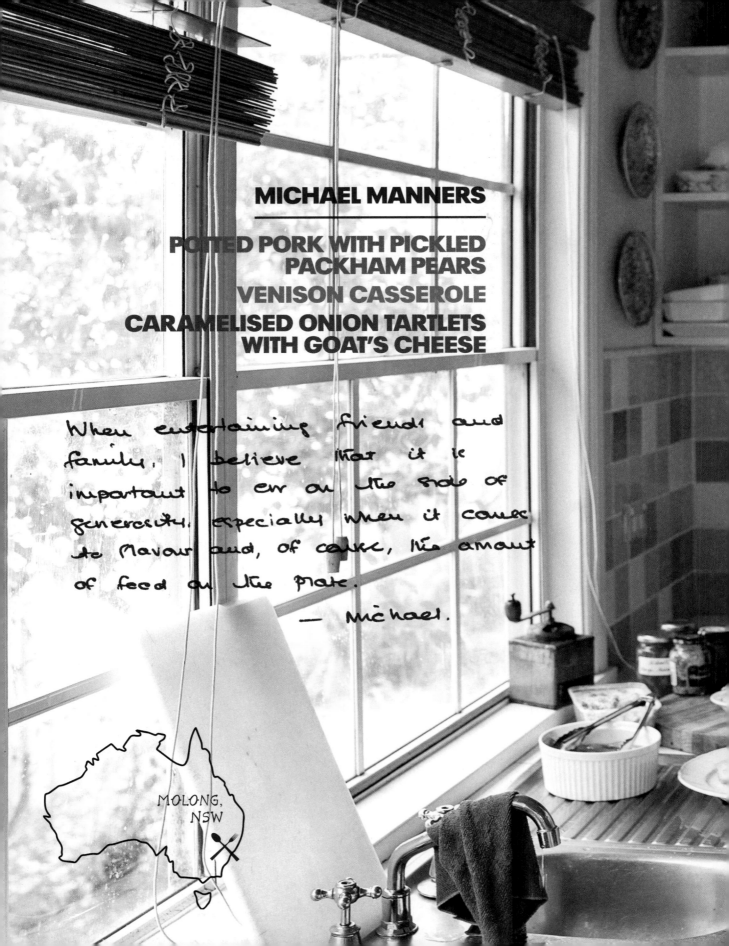

MICHAEL MANNERS

POTTED PORK WITH PICKLED PACKHAM PEARS
VENISON CASSEROLE
CARAMELISED ONION TARTLETS WITH GOAT'S CHEESE

When entertaining friends and family, I believe that it is important to err on the side of generosity, especially when it comes to flavour and, of course, the amount of food on the plate.

— Michael.

MOLONG, NSW

POTTED PORK WITH PICKLED PACKHAM PEARS

SERVINGS: 16–20 | PREP TIME: 1 HOUR PLUS MARINATING
COOK TIME: UP TO 2 HOURS | SKILL LEVEL: 2 (MODERATE)

INGREDIENTS

Pork rillettes

1 kg fatty pork belly
2 tsp salt
½ tsp pepper
pinch of freshly
   ground nutmeg
2 cloves garlic, diced
2–3 sprigs of fresh thyme
2 fresh bay leaves
1 brown onion, diced
olive oil
100 ml dry white wine
100 ml chicken stock

Pickled pears

1 cup honey
1 cup white vinegar
3 Packham pears (because
   I'm from Molong, where
   Packhams originated)
1 cinnamon quill
15 black peppercorns
4 cloves
1 bay leaf

METHOD

For the rillettes: remove the skin from the pork belly and dice the flesh into 3 cm cubes. Place the cubes in a mixing bowl and add the salt, pepper, nutmeg, garlic and the thyme and bay leaves. Cover the bowl and place it in the fridge to marinate for at least 4 hours; overnight is better.

Remove the pork cubes from the fridge and pre-heat the oven to 150°C. In an ovenproof pan on a medium to high heat, sweat the onion in a little olive oil, then add the pork and sauté until the pinkness goes from the meat, but do not let the pork brown. Add the wine and stock and bring to the boil. Remove the pan from the heat, cover with a lid or tinfoil and place in the oven for 1–2 hours or until the pork is really well cooked. (You can also cook the rillettes in a pressure cooker, allowing 40 minutes from the time the pot comes up to pressure.)

Allow the rillettes to cool a little, remove the thyme and bay leaves, strain most of the fat off and mix with a fork until the meat is well shredded and free of lumps. Mix the fat back in and store in sterilised jars in the fridge for up to a week. Rillettes can be frozen for up to three months; I divide it into 200 g containers (a serving is 40–60 g per person).

For the pears: whisk together the honey and vinegar in a saucepan on a medium heat. Taste the mixture and adjust as needed. The idea is to have a balanced sweet-and-sour mix, but do allow for some sweetness from the fruit during cooking.

Peel, core and slice the pears. Add the spices, bay leaf and pears to the honey and vinegar and cook gently until the pears are soft but not breaking apart; cooking time will vary depending on the pears, so check regularly. Remove the pan from the heat and set aside to cool completely. Store in a sterilised jar or container in the fridge for up to a week.

Serve the rillettes on mini-toasts with the pear slices, or as part of an antipasti or charcuterie plate.

VENISON CASSEROLE
A MEDIEVAL RECIPE

SERVINGS: 6 | PREP TIME: 20 MINS | COOK TIME: 2 HOURS | SKILL LEVEL: 1 (EASY)

INGREDIENTS

1 kg venison shoulder
 (I use Mandagery
 Creek venison)
2 tsp ground black
 peppercorns
½ tsp freshly ground
 nutmeg
1 tsp allspice
1 cinnamon quill
2 tsp ground coriander
1 tsp salt flakes
2 large brown onions,
 peeled and sliced
juice and zest of 1 orange
450 ml beef stock
1 cup dried apricots
1 cup pitted prunes
⅔ cup raisins
salt and pepper

(DF) (GF)

METHOD

Pre-heat the oven to 150°C. Dice the venison into 3 cm cubes. In a mixing bowl, combine the cubed venison with the spices and salt flakes. Use your hands to mix everything well. Heat a stovetop- and oven-proof dish on the stove to a medium-high heat, and brown the seasoned venison until the meat is sealed. Add the onions and stir thoroughly to combine. Add in the orange juice and zest, as well as the stock, and bring the liquid to the boil.

Remove the dish from the heat, cover it well with tinfoil or a tight-fitting lid and place the dish in the oven for an hour. After the hour, remove the from the oven, add in the fruit and continue to cook for an hour or so, until the meat is tender. Taste and adjust the seasoning. Serve with mashed potatoes or noodles and a green salad.

CARAMELISED ONION TARTLETS
WITH GOAT'S CHEESE

SERVINGS: 4 | PREP TIME: 20 MINS | COOK TIME: 5 MINS | SKILL LEVEL: 1 (EASY)

INGREDIENTS

4 tbsp olive oil
100 g butter
4–5 large onions, peeled
 and finely sliced
salt and pepper to taste
a few sprigs of fresh thyme
a dash of balsamic vinegar
4 store-bought pastry
 shells or home-made
 pre-cooked tartlets
1 log soft goat's cheese
 (approx. 160 g)

(V)

METHOD

In a pan on a medium heat, combine the oil and butter until melted and then add the onion. Season with salt and pepper and a few sprigs of fresh thyme. Once the onion starts to brown, turn the heat down to low and cook gently to allow the onion to lightly caramelise. When the onion is soft and golden and sweet, add a dash of balsamic vinegar to heighten the taste.

To serve, pre-heat an oven to 180°C. Fill the tart shells with the onion and top with a few dots of goat's cheese – you can use more or less, as you prefer. Season with salt and pepper, a few fresh thyme leaves and a splash of fruity olive oil. Warm the tarts in the oven for about 5 minutes, or until hot.

TIP

For variation, before cooking the tarts you can add white anchovy fillets, and/or tomatoes when they are in season and full of flavour.

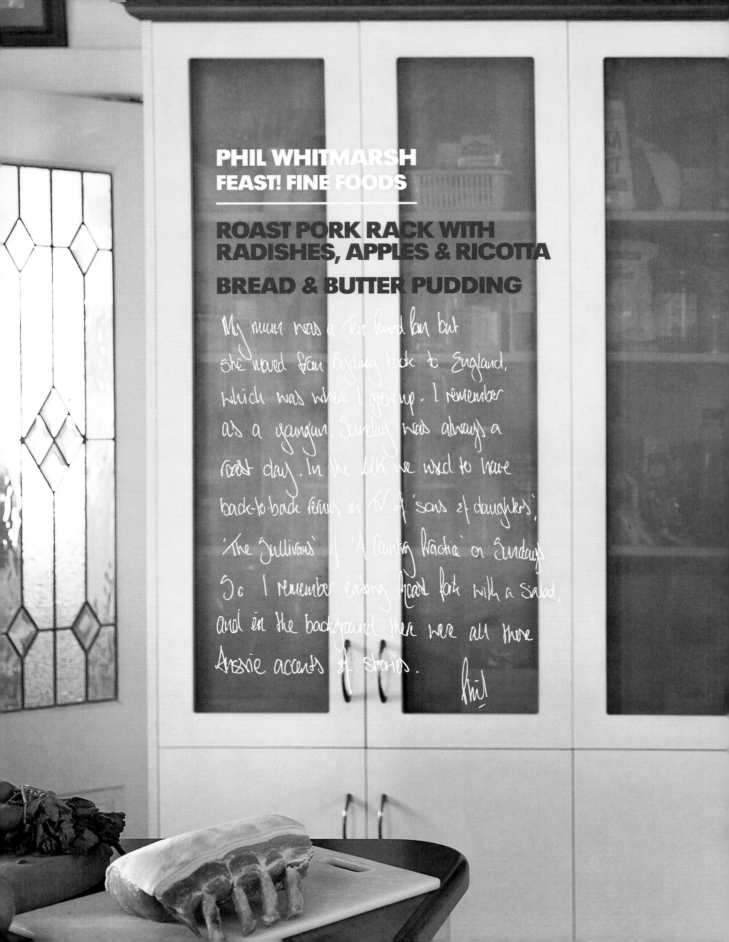

PHIL WHITMARSH
FEAST! FINE FOODS

ROAST PORK RACK WITH RADISHES, APPLES & RICOTTA

BREAD & BUTTER PUDDING

My mum was a Ten Pound Pom but she moved from Sydney back to England, which was where I grew up. I remember as a youngun, Sunday was always a roast day. In the UK we used to have back-to-back reruns on TV of 'sons & daughters', 'The Sullivans' & 'A Country Practice' on Sundays. So I remember eating Roast Pork with a salad, and in the background there were all those Aussie accents & stories.

Phil

SEACLIFF, SA

ROAST PORK RACK WITH RADISHES, APPLES & RICOTTA

SERVINGS: 8 | PREP TIME: 1 HOUR PLUS DRYING AND DRAINING
COOK TIME: APPROX. 1 HOUR | SKILL LEVEL: 1 (EASY)

INGREDIENTS

1 rack of a good
 breed of pork
 (I use Berkshire pork)

Salad

1 daikon radish

3 black radishes

2 watermelon radishes

3 large red radishes

5 pink radishes

5 purple radishes

2 Pink Lady apples

2 Granny Smith apples

1 bunch chives

2 tbsp olive oil (approx.)

juice of 2 lemons

Ricotta

2 litres best cow's milk
 money can buy

500 ml double cream

75 g lemon juice
 or white vinegar

9 g (or 1.75 tsp) salt

METHOD

Right, for the pork, first things first, you're gonna want (need) crackling, so unwrap your rack and place it on a plate or whatever in the fridge. You need that skin to dry out a bit, so leave it for a few hours. When that's all done, take it out of the fridge and let it get to room temperature.

Crank the oven up to 220°C, probably 200°C for fan-forced. Season just the meat (not the skin) — I use salt and pepper, but if you fancy it then chuck on some spices and/or herbs too. Place the pork, skin-side up, in a roasting tray and put it in the oven; give it 20 minutes and then drop the temp to 180°C (160°C for fan-forced), and continue cooking for another 35–45 minutes. Take your now gloriously crackling-covered rack out of the oven and give it a probe with a meat thermometer; I usually take her out when she's hit 60°C. Let your rack rest somewhere warm — don't cover it, though, or your crackling will sweat and go soggy, and no one likes soggy crackling!

The salad is literally the easiest salad you'll ever make. Slice all the radishes and apples wafer-thin on a Japanese mandolin and place in a huge bowl — you need room to get your hands in there in a bit. If there's any nice delicate leaves on your radishes, give them a wash and throw them into your bowl too. Chop your chives nice and fine, place over the apples and radishes, and season it all with salt and pepper. Now pour over your oil and lemon juice, as much as your heart desires. Get involved with your hands and make sure everything is dressed properly.

Ricotta — this makes a shit-load! It's heaps easier if you've got a probe thermometer. Heat your milk and cream together until it hits 85°C. Remove from the heat and quickly add in the lemon juice or vinegar along with the salt — give it a real good whisk and then cover and let it sit for 20–30 minutes. Line a colander with muslin or paper towel, set it over a bucket or bowl and pour your milk mix into it. Let it hang for about 1 hour. I like my ricotta quite wet, so an hour will do for me.

To serve, carve up your rack, one bone per person. Dollop a good spoonful of ricotta onto each plate, cover that with your radish and apple salad, place a piece of pork next to it, and serve.

BREAD & BUTTER PUDDING

SERVINGS: 6 | PREP TIME: 45 MINS | COOK TIME: 30 MINS | SKILL LEVEL: 1 (EASY)

INGREDIENTS

60 ml (double shot) whiskey, rum, brandy or bourbon (optional)

60 g sultanas

60 g raisins

12 slices of good bread that's a few days old

butter, as much or as little as you like

600 ml full-fat milk

600 ml full-fat cream

2 vanilla pods, split in half lengthways

12 egg yolks

250 g caster sugar, plus extra for caramelising

METHOD

If you're using the booze, soak your fruits in it while you work on the rest.

Pre-heat the oven to 180°C.

Butter your bread – be as generous or as 'economical' as you wish. I like heaps of butter, but each to their own.

Heat your milk and cream with the split vanilla pods until almost boiling. While that's doing its thing, whisk up your yolks and sugar. When your milk mix is hot, gently pour half over the eggs while whisking like a lunatic, then pour this back into the rest of the milk mix. Stir over the heat for another minute or two – this is custard. Remove it from the heat.

If you've used the booze to soak your fruit in, drain the fruit in a sieve and put the excess booze into your custard. Let the custard cool down (or if you've got chef's hands, don't wait), and dip the buttered bread into the custard, then lay it into a deepish baking dish. When the first layer is done, chuck over some of your fruit; keep going on this tangent until you've run out of bread and fruit. Don't put any fruit on top, though, as it'll burn and not be very delicious.

There should be a fair whack of custard left over. I like to pour it over the bread until it's barely covered and let it stand for about 5–10 minutes; this lets your bread soak up all that custard. Now bake in the oven for about 20–30 minutes; you want your custard to wobble a bit. If it's too firm, it's over; if it's too wobbly, give it a bit longer.

When it's done, let it hang out on the side to rest for about 10–15 minutes. When that's done, give it a liberal sprinkling of caster sugar and caramelise the top with a blow-torch or under a hot grill; this will give you a nice crème brûlée-type crunch on top. Spoon out into bowls and serve with more custard if you want.

If you fancy it, you can also spread Nutella or jam or marmalade on your bread, too. Either way, it's bloody glorious!

ANGIE & DAN HONG

CHẢ GIÒ
BÁNH HỎI CHẠO TÔM

Going to my mum's house for Monday Hong Dinners Is the highlight of my week. I rarely say yes to going out with mates for dinner that night because I know that no meal will ever be as good as the one I share with my family at that table.

Dan Hong

NEWTOWN,
NSW

CHẢ GIÒ
VIETNAMESE SPRING ROLLS

MAKES: 60 | PREP TIME: 30 MINS | COOK TIME: 20–30 MINS | SKILL LEVEL: 2 (MODERATE)

INGREDIENTS

Filling
500 g minced pork neck
½ cup water chestnuts, finely chopped
½ cup of each of the following, all shredded:
  wood ear mushrooms
  shiitake mushrooms
  carrot
  onion
  mung bean thread
  (1 cm lengths, softened in cold water)

Seasoning
2 tsp table salt
4 tsp raw sugar
1 tsp ground white pepper

To finish
1 tbsp dark soy sauce
1 packet medium-sized rice paper wrappers
vegetable oil for deep-frying

METHOD

In a mixing bowl, combine the filling ingredients with the seasonings and mix thoroughly.

Carefully pour hot water into a shallow, wide dish along with the soy sauce. Stir to combine. Take a rice paper wrapper and quickly immerse it in the hot water, then place on a clean, dry plate. Spoon a tablespoon of the mixture into the centre of the rice paper in a sausage shape. Fold the top and bottom ends in, then roll the rice paper up like a cigar. Set aside and repeat until all of the mixture has been used up.

Heat the oil in a heavy-based pot until it reaches 180°C. In small batches, fry the spring rolls for 7–10 minutes or until the outside is crisp and golden. Drain onto paper towel and serve hot with your favourite dipping sauce.

BÁNH HỎI CHẠO TÔM
SUGAR CANE PRAWN RICE PAPER ROLLS

MAKES: 12 | PREP TIME: 1 HOUR | SKILL LEVEL: 2 (MODERATE)

INGREDIENTS

1 kg black tiger prawn meat
  (frozen is better in this case)
2 cloves garlic, finely minced
2 tsp table salt
5 tsp raw sugar
1 tsp ground white pepper
1 tsp baking powder
½ cup arrowroot flour
Canned or fresh sugar cane,
  cut into 20 cm lengths approx. 1 cm in
  diameter (kind of like a stick of cabanossi)
vegetable oil for deep-frying

To serve
1 bunch each of your favourite Vietnamese herbs,
  e.g. perilla, Vietnamese mint and garden mint
1 butter lettuce, torn into leaves
1 Lebanese cucumber, sliced into sticks
1 handful mung bean sprouts, washed
Nước chaắm dipping sauce
Vietnamese pickled carrots and daikon
1 packet rice vermicelli noodles, cooked
1 packet rice paper sheets

METHOD

In a large mixing bowl, combine the frozen prawns with the garlic, salt, sugar, pepper, baking powder and arrowroot flour. Refrigerate the mixture for 1 hour, then transfer the contents to a food processor and blitz until a smooth paste is formed. Divide this prawn mousse into balls the size of tennis balls. On a clean, slightly damp surface, pound each ball several times to eliminate air pockets. Once pounded, wrap the prawn mousse around a stick of sugar cane and repeat until all of the mousse has been used up.

Transfer the sugar cane prawns to a steamer basket, and steam for 20 minutes or until the prawn mousse is firm. These can be stored in the freezer and thawed out as needed. Heat a deep-fryer or a heavy-based pot of oil to 180°C and fry the sugar cane prawns in batches until golden. Alternatively, they can be barbecued or grilled until heated through.

To serve: arrange the herbs and salad ingredients on several big plates, along with the fried sugar cane prawns (you can slide off the sugar cane and split into four, lengthways), pickles, rice noodles and the uncooked rice paper. Pour hot water into shallow, wide bowls within reach of each person.

To eat, each person dips a sheet of rice paper into hot water, places it on a plate, and adds their own preference of fillings to the centre. Roll up like a cigar or burrito, dip in nước chaắm and enjoy!

SARAH SWAN & JEREMY BURN
100 MILE TABLE

GRANOLA
MANDARIN MARMALADE
BACON & EGG BUTTY

It's a nice little bit of rebellion, making bacon & egg butties around here. Byron Bay is a wonderful town of hippies and chia seeds and gluten free organics and that's important. But we like bacon. And eggs. And organic food. And chia seeds. we just don't do so many. — Sarah & Jeremy

BYRON BAY,
NSW

GRANOLA

MAKES: APPROX. 1.5 KG | PREP TIME: 5 MINS | COOK TIME: 25–35 MINS | SKILL LEVEL: 1 (EASY)

INGREDIENTS

2½ tbsp coconut oil
½ cup real maple syrup
3 tbsp honey
1 tsp vanilla essence
350 g rolled oats
60 g sunflower seeds
60 g pumpkin seeds
30 g sesame seeds
60 g shredded coconut
300 g dried blueberries
400 g dried pears,
 sliced thinly

METHOD

Pre-heat the oven to 160°C.

Add the coconut oil, maple syrup, honey and vanilla to a large mixing bowl and mix well. Add the oats and seeds and mix well to combine.

Transfer the granola mix to a baking tray and place in the oven. Cook until golden, (about 20–30 minutes) stirring well every 5 minutes or so because it will cook faster around the edges than on the inside.

When just golden, add the coconut and return to the oven for a final 5 minutes.

Remove the granola from the oven and mix the blueberries and sliced pear through.

When cool, store in airtight jars. Serve with your favourite milk, yoghurt and fresh seasonal fruit or fruit compote.

TIP

This is a very straightforward recipe that enables you to have home-made granola at home all the time. Feel free to swap out any of the seeds for extra dried fruit or nuts, or change it around with each fresh batch. We also love to use dried peaches, pineapple or apricots, and macadamias and pistachios are a great addition too.

MANDARIN MARMALADE

MAKES: ABOUT 2.5 KG | PREP TIME: 5 MINS | COOK TIME: 1–1½ HOURS | SKILL LEVEL: 1 (EASY)

INGREDIENTS

12 whole sweet
  mandarins, skin on
juice of 4 lemons
  (plus extra to taste)
caster sugar as
  needed
  (1 kg–1.3kg)

METHOD

Put the mandarins and lemon juice into a large pot big enough to hold them all. Just cover the fruit with cold water, place over a medium-high heat and bring to the boil. Once boiling, reduce to a gentle simmer and cook until the mandarins are completely soft and just starting to break apart (about 30 minutes). Remove the mandarins from the pot (retain the liquid) and set about removing the seeds. While they are still hot, I do this by tearing them apart with two pairs of small tongs and just lifting the seeds out – not a painful exercise but it does take a little patience. Discard the seeds.

Purée all the remaining mandarin pieces, skin and all, in a blender. It doesn't need to be completely smooth – you will still see pieces of skin and flesh (it's marmalade, after all!). Add the purée back to the water and measure the fruit and water mixture combined. You are now going to add exactly the same amount of sugar to this mixture, so if you have 1 litre of fruit/water, then add 1 kg of sugar.

Place the pot back on a medium-high heat and bring to the boil, stirring all the time to dissolve the sugar. When the sugar has dissolved, taste the marmalade for balance; I like it to be really citrusy so at this point will often add extra lemon juice – 2 or 3 lemons usually does the trick and lime juice works well too. Keeping it on a steady, constant boil, cook for about 30 minutes and then do the 'flake test': when you are close to setting point, take a tablespoon of the jam or marmalade with a metal spoon and leave it to cool a little. Now tilt the spoon on its side and pour the mixture onto a plate. If the marmalade drips in a solid sheet, it is ready. If it falls in drips, then you are not quite there yet. Make sure to remove the pot from the heat while you test, so that it doesn't over-boil.

Once the setting point is reached, remove the marmalade from the heat and leave to cool for 10 minutes before pouring into hot, sterilised jars. Seal straight away.

BACON & EGG BUTTY

SERVINGS: 4 | PREP TIME: 15–20 MINS | SKILL LEVEL: 1 (EASY)

INGREDIENTS

4 medium-sized rolls
  (we like corn rolls)
4 rashers organic bacon,
  rind removed
4 whole organic eggs
4 tbsp tomato relish or
  good-quality chutney
4 tbsp Green Goddess
  dressing

*Green Goddess dressing
(makes 1½ cups)*
1 cup mayonnaise
½ cup sour cream
juice of 1 lemon
1 small clove garlic
1 cup herb leaves, finely
  chopped (we use parsley
  and tarragon with a
  little sage, oregano
  and marjoram)
3 tbsp finely chopped chives

METHOD

Slice the rolls in half, and toast – we toast on the cut side only, then warm the tops and bottoms with the roof of the sandwich press, but you can do this however you want. Let's face it, it's not rocket science. If you are making this for breakfast at home, I would do the whole lot on the barbecue.

Meanwhile, pop your bacon rashers on to cook, followed closely by the eggs. I like to break the yolks with a single stab from a fork and then keep the eggs contained by 'rounding them up' to get an even egg that isn't going to run out as soon as you bite into it. That said, do remove the egg before it goes hard.

To make the Green Goddess dressing, mix the mayonnaise and sour cream together until smooth. Add the lemon juice and whisk to combine. Finely crush the garlic and add with all the chopped herbs, then season with sea salt and freshly ground pepper to taste. Keeps covered in the fridge for up to three days.

Spread the tomato relish or chutney over the toasted bottoms of the four rolls and spread Green Goddess over the tops. Place an egg on top of the relish, followed by the bacon, with each rasher curled into a roll. Add the top half to each roll and serve.

Both these dishes have a familiarity
about them; they feel like old friends. Pizza
and even spaghetti and meatballs (which is
American, not Italian), belong to the world
now and everyone has a version of them.
That's what keeps cuisine going. That's why
you cook. Because you're trying to perfect
a recipe for the people you love.
— Stefano

STEFANO MANFREDI

PIZZA IN TEGLIA
BUCATINI ALL'AMERICANA

CAMPERDOWN,
NSW

PIZZA IN TEGLIA
ROMAN-STYLE PIZZA WITH PROSCIUTTO, BURRATA & EGGPLANT

SERVINGS: 4 | PREP TIME: 40 MINS PLUS RISING | SKILL LEVEL: 2 (MODERATE)

INGREDIENTS

Pizza base (makes three 550 g sheets or teglie)

1 kg strong bread flour, preferably stoneground

3.5 g powdered yeast

650 g water, warmed to about 30°C

½ tsp caster sugar

27 ml extra virgin olive oil

20 g sea salt

Topping

8 squares of Roman teglia (each side 8 cm)

8 thin slices prosciutto di Parma or similar

8 thin slices grilled eggplant

1 or 2 burrata (see note), depending on size (or mozzarella if burrata is unavailable)

METHOD

Make the dough the day before you want the pizzas. Place the flour in the bowl of a stand mixer and attach a dough hook. Dissolve the yeast in 100 ml of the water and add to the flour, along with 400 ml of the remaining water as well as the sugar. Turn the mixer to low and mix until the water is totally absorbed and the dough is beginning to stretch and form long gluten strands. Add the oil and salt and mix in. Increase the speed of the mixer and slowly add the remaining 150 ml of water a little at a time, adding more only when the previous amount has been absorbed. Place the dough in an oiled plastic tub, rub your hands with extra virgin olive oil and place them under the outer edges of the dough, sliding them under to form a ball. Repeat a couple of times until the dough has a ball-like appearance. Cover the container with an airtight lid and leave overnight in the fridge.

Next day, remove the dough from the container and divide into three. Place each piece on a separate oiled baking tray, and fit to the tray by placing your fingers under each side and gently stretching the dough, or by rolling with a rolling pin. Leave for a couple of hours to rise.

Meanwhile, pre-heat the oven to 250°C (non-fan-forced). Bake in the oven for 11–12 minutes. If the teglia is browning more on one side, your oven is not even and the tray may need to be turned around. Once cooked, remove from the oven and leave to cool completely. The teglia is now ready to use, or you can wrap it tightly with plastic wrap and store in the refrigerator for up to three days.

When ready to make the pizza, pre-heat the oven to 180°C. Cut your 8 cm squares from one teglia, place on a baking tray and heat in the oven until they are crisp on the outside but soft in the middle. This will take about 5–6 minutes. Meanwhile, make sure all the other ingredients are ready. Prosciutto should be sliced. Eggplant slices should be hot. Cut burrata into eight pieces in a bowl, using a sharp knife. The burrata will fall apart because it is soft. Once the teglia is ready, remove from the oven. Form a cup using a piece of grilled eggplant in the middle and a slice of prosciutto on the outside. Place this neatly on each of the teglie and arrange on serving plates. Spoon the burrata into the middle of the cup. Season lightly with salt and freshly cracked pepper and serve immediately.

BUCATINI ALL'AMERICANA
SPAGHETTI & MEATBALLS

SERVINGS: 6–8 | PREP TIME: 45–60 MINS | COOK TIME: 15–20 MINS | SKILL LEVEL: 1 (EASY)

INGREDIENTS

Tomato salsa (makes 500 ml)

4 tbsp extra virgin olive oil

1 medium-sized onion,
  finely diced

2 cloves garlic, peeled
  and minced

1 small leek, trimmed and
  cut into fine half-rounds

1 stick celery from the
  heart, finely chopped

650 g Italian peeled
  tomatoes, mashed

1 tsp fennel seeds

Meatballs

500 g lean pork shoulder

100 g pork fat

100 g mortadella

100 g day-old bread,
  crusts removed

⅓ cup milk

1 tsp finely chopped thyme

1 tbsp finely chopped sage

2 tbsp finely chopped parsley

2 tbsp minced garlic

1 tsp ground nutmeg

100 g grated Parmesan,
  plus extra to serve

1 egg

plain flour, for rolling

80 g bucatini per person

METHOD

Heat olive oil in a pan and gently fry onion, garlic, leek and celery until transparent. Add tomato and fennel seeds. Season with a couple of pinches of salt and some pepper. Stir well, and simmer until sauce thickens and most of the water has evaporated.

Mince together pork, pork fat and mortadella using a hand or an electric mincer. Soak bread in milk until milk is mostly absorbed. Add bread, minus any milk that's not absorbed, to mince mixture along with herbs, garlic, nutmeg, Parmesan and egg. Mix well with your hands, taking care to incorporate all the ingredients. Add salt and pepper to taste. A good way to taste for seasoning is to fry a small patty made from the mixture in a little olive oil; adjust if necessary.

Roll mixture into meatballs the diameter of a 20-cent piece, lightly flouring your hands so they don't stick. Once all the meatballs are ready, poach them in lightly simmering tomato sauce for 15–20 minutes. (Any leftover meatballs can be frozen, tightly sealed on a tray.)

Cook the bucatini to al dente according to packet instructions, and serve tossed gently with the meatballs. Sprinkle with Parmesan to taste.

TIPS

The pork fat called for is the sort that goes into making sausages and salami so succulent. Ask your butcher.

Bucatini are thick spaghetti with a hole in the middle. I think that thicker-gauge long pasta works better with the meatballs.

TARA & JEFF LEONG
THE NUTRITION GURU AND THE CHEF

PUMPKIN SALAD WITH FETA, SUNFLOWER SEEDS & WALNUTS
CHOC MOUSSE SLICE
MILK JELLIES

Don't get involved in food fads of "you should be eating this, you shouldn't be eating that." It can be easy to get bogged down by that, and feel you have to go out and buy expensive ingredients.

The best tip is to eat fresh; lots of fruit and vegetables. Use that idea as a base and you're on your way to good health. — Tara

NOOSA, QLD

PUMPKIN SALAD WITH FETA, SUNFLOWER SEEDS & WALNUTS

SERVINGS: 4 | PREP TIME: 20 MINS | COOK TIME: 1 HOUR | SKILL LEVEL: 1 (EASY)

INGREDIENTS

Salad

1 medium pumpkin
  (or approx. 8 cups)
2 large red onions
30 ml olive oil
100 g mild feta
1 cup pumpkin seeds
1 cup sunflower seeds
1 cup roughly chopped
  walnuts
olive oil

Dressing

3 tbsp chutney (e.g. mango)
2 tbsp wholegrain mustard
3 tbsp extra virgin olive oil

METHOD

Pre-heat the oven to 180°C.

Remove the skin from the pumpkin using a sharp knife, and chop into bite-sized pieces. Chop the onion into similar-sized pieces. Place the pumpkin and onions on a large baking tray that has been lined with non-stick baking paper. Drizzle with olive oil and season to taste.

Bake in the oven for 30 minutes, then turn oven off and let the vegetables sit for another 30 minutes to cook through and soften.

Meanwhile, make the dressing: mix the chutney, mustard and olive oil together in a small bowl until well incorporated. Set aside.

Remove vegetables from the oven and allow to cool. When they are cool, mix half the dressing mixture through them. Reserve the rest of the dressing to serve to the side of the dish.

To serve, pile the dressed pumpkin and onion onto a large serving plate, drizzling with any leftover oil from the baking tray. Crumble the feta over the top, along with the sunflower seeds, pumpkin seeds and walnuts, and drizzle with olive oil. Place the reserved dressing in a small jug to the side.

CHOC MOUSSE SLICE

SERVINGS: 12 | PREP TIME: 30 MINS PLUS CHILLING | SKILL LEVEL: 1 (EASY)

INGREDIENTS

Base

1 cup almonds
½ cup sunflower seeds
½ cup sesame seeds
½ cup sultanas or dates
1 tbsp coconut oil or water

Filling

2 ripe bananas
4 tbsp tahini or soft
  unsalted nut butter
¼ cup gluten-free cocoa
4 tbsp maple syrup
  or 2 tbsp honey
2 tbsp chia seeds

Ganache

1 cup gluten-free cocoa
1 cup water
4 tbsp honey
  or maple syrup
4 tbsp olive, coconut
  or sunflower oil

METHOD

For the base: throw everything in the blender. Blend until combined. Remove the lid of the blender and scrape down the sides from time to time to make sure the mixture continues to break down. The oils will start to release and make the mixture stick together. Keep blending until it does so. If the mixture is still too crumbly, add 1 extra tbsp of water and continue to blend.

Line a loaf tin with non-stick baking paper. Press the base mixture over the bottom of the tin and place in the freezer to set for 1 hour.

For the filling: place all ingredients in a blender and blend until smooth. Remove the base from the freezer and pour the filling mixture on top, to cover the base. Place back in the freezer for at least 4 hours, or overnight, to set.

For the ganache: place all ingredients except oil in a small saucepan on a high heat, stirring to combine. Let mixture bubble for 5 minutes, stirring to keep it from sticking to the bottom of the pan. Once mixture is starting to thicken, add oil and stir vigorously to incorporate. Remove from the heat and allow to cool.

Once cool, remove the slice from the freezer and pour the ganache over the top to cover. Use a spatula to smooth it over. Return to the freezer to set. Slice to serve.

TIP

All elements of this slice can be served on their own: the mousse layer is perfect served in glasses, the base mixture is perfect rolled into bliss balls, and the ganache is a healthy addition for topping any cake or pancakes.

MILK JELLIES

SERVINGS: 4 | PREP TIME: 30 MINS PLUS CHILLING | SKILL LEVEL: 2 (MODERATE)

INGREDIENTS

1¼ tsp powdered gelatine (measure this very accurately)

100 ml warm water

1 cup milk

1 cup natural yoghurt

2 tbsp liquid honey or maple syrup

seasonal fresh fruit

METHOD

In a cup, sprinkle the gelatine over the warm water. Let the gelatine soak into the water for 5 minutes.

In the meantime, bring the milk to the boil in a saucepan on a medium heat. Once the milk reaches the boil, quickly remove the pan from the heat and set aside.

Using a spoon, stir the gelatine and water mixture to combine. The gelatine will have absorbed all the water and have become a paste.

Spoon the gelatine mixture into the hot milk, while quickly whisking the mixture to dissolve the gelatine. It is important to whisk quickly here to stop the gelatine from clumping together.

Leave the mixture to cool, approximately 15 minutes (this step is important to prevent curdling). When cool, whisk in the yoghurt until well combined. If mixture splits, this is because the milk was too hot. This is OK – simply place mixture in a blender and blend for 30 seconds.

Pour mixture into four individual plastic wine glasses, dariole moulds or any vessel you wish to serve them in. Cover each with plastic wrap to prevent the top from hardening. Place in fridge overnight or for at least 3 hours.

To serve, drizzle with honey or maple syrup and top with fresh fruit.

**JON HEALEY
PYENGANA DAIRY COMPANY**

**BEEF & CHEDDAR POT PIE
CHEESY CHIVE SCONES**

I NEVER USED TO SLEEP AT ALL. I WOULD TRANSPORT THE MILK TO THE CHEESE FACTORY AND DO FOUR OR FIVE TRIPS A DAY, AND AFTER THAT, GET IN A LITTLE MILK TRUCK AND TRAVEL 650km AROUND THE NORTH OF THE STATE, DELIVERING MILK. MY MOTHER ASKED ME TO STOP WHEN ONE DAY I FELL ASLEEP AT THE WHEEL AND CRASHED THE TRUCK IN THE MAIN STREET OF LAUNCESTON. THEY SAY YOU SHOULDN'T CRY OVER SPILT MILK, BUT I RECKON THAT DAY, I DID.

Jon

PYENGANA, TAS

BEEF & CHEDDAR POT PIE

SERVINGS: 6 | PREP TIME: 30 MINS | COOK TIME: 1½ HOURS | SKILL LEVEL: 1 (EASY)

INGREDIENTS

2 tbsp vegetable oil

1 kg diced beef topside

1 medium brown onion, peeled and chopped

2 carrots, peeled and chopped

2 sticks celery, trimmed and chopped

2 cloves garlic, crushed

300 g canned crushed tomatoes

2 cups beef stock

2 medium potatoes, peeled and chopped

½ cup butter

⅔ cup plain flour

150 g Pyengana cheddar, grated

3 sheets frozen shortcrust pastry, thawed

spray oil

METHOD

Pre-heat oven to 220°C (200°C fan-forced).

Heat 1 tbsp oil in a large, heavy-based saucepan over a medium-high heat. Cook beef, in batches, until browned all over. Transfer to a bowl.

Heat remaining oil in pan. Add onion, carrot, celery and garlic. Cook, stirring, for about 2 minutes or until vegetables are soft. Return beef and juices to pan. Add tomato and stir to combine. Add stock. Cover and bring to the boil. Reduce heat to low and simmer for 40 minutes or until beef is half tender.

Add potato when meat starts to become tender. Simmer for another 20 minutes, until potato is cooked.

Meanwhile, melt butter in a small saucepan over a medium-low heat, add flour and stir until combined well. Add to pie mix to thicken. Then add cheese, and season with salt and pepper.

Line the bottom of a deep pie dish with 2 sheets of pastry. Fill with beef mixture. Top with remaining pastry sheet. Lightly spray pastry with oil. Bake for 15 minutes or until pastry is golden. Serve with relish of your choice.

CHEESY CHIVE SCONES

MAKES: 48 | PREP TIME: 15 MINS | COOK TIME: 14–18 MINS PER TRAY | SKILL LEVEL: 1 (EASY)

INGREDIENTS

900 g self-raising flour

80 g grated Pyengana cheddar

½ handful dried chive flakes (I use the Chinese variety)

315 ml cream

315 ml soda water

METHOD

Pre-heat oven to 230°C (210°C fan-forced). Line baking trays with baking paper.

Sift flour into a bowl. Add cheese and chive flakes.

Make a well in centre of the mixture. Add cream and soda water. Using a wooden spoon, stir until a sticky dough forms. Turn out onto a lightly floured surface. Knead gently until just smooth.

Using a lightly floured rolling pin, gently roll dough out until 4 cm thick. Using a 7 cm round cutter, cut out scones. Press leftover dough together. Repeat to make 48 scones.

Place scones, just touching, on prepared trays. Bake each tray for 11–13 minutes or until golden, then turn temperature down to 190°C and cook for another 3–5 minutes, until cooked inside or an inserted skewer comes out clean.

VICTOR & EVELYN LIONG
LEE HO FOOK

SWEET & SOUR PORK
FRIED RICE
BARLEY TONIC

We don't really have that many days off together,
but when we do, it generally involves eating. We'll
go out to eat dumplings, noodles, spicy Schuan food
and there's always a drink or two involved.
Working together as siblings can get a little tough,
but it's nice to take a few minutes to debrief, and
then we don't talk about work. We're siblings again.

— Victor + Ev

COLLINGWOOD, VIC

SWEET & SOUR PORK

SERVINGS: 4 | PREP TIME: 3½ HOURS PLUS MARINATING
COOK TIME: 20 MINS PLUS SAUCE MAKING | SKILL LEVEL: 1 (EASY)

INGREDIENTS

Sweet and sour sauce
100 g onions, sliced
20 g long red chillies, sliced
40 g cloves garlic, smashed
80 ml vegetable oil for cooking
125 g strawberries, sliced
500 ml chicken stock
120 ml white vinegar
25 ml Japanese soy sauce
130 g sugar
40 ml Shaoxing rice wine
120 ml Heinz Big Red Tomato Sauce
100 g pineapple, diced

Marinade
50 ml Japanese soy sauce
50 ml Shaoxing rice wine
15 g chicken stock powder
20 g sugar
1 tsp salt
2 tsp sesame oil
⅛ tsp (1 g) five-spice powder
5 g (1 clove) garlic, microplaned

Pork
300 g organic pork neck,
  cut into 1½ cm cubes
oil for deep-frying

Starch mix
100 g rice flour
100 g tapioca starch

To finish
20 g long red chillies, sliced thinly
20 g spring onions, cut into batons
10 g pineapple, diced finely
10 g carrot, sliced thinly
30 g kuzu starch
  (available in any Japanese
  or specialist Asian grocer)
40 ml cold water

METHOD

For the sauce: stir-fry onion, chilli and garlic in the oil in a wok until caramelised, then add remaining ingredients and cook on a simmer for at least 3 hours, or until the strawberries have lost their vibrant red colour and have begun to turn white. Strain and cool.

For the pork: mix all marinade ingredients together until dissolved. Marinate the pork neck cubes in the marinade for at least 6 hours.

Place oil in a deep pan and heat to 180°C. Drain pork of excess marinade, dredge in starch mix until well coated, and deep-fry for 3–4 minutes, until pork is cooked.

To finish: stir-fry vegetables in a little oil until aromatic. Add sweet and sour sauce and bring to the boil, then thicken with a slurry of kuzu starch mixed with water. Add pork. Stir-fry until pork is coated in sauce and serve immediately.

FRIED RICE

SERVINGS: 4 | PREP TIME: 45 MINS PLUS DRYING OVERNIGHT
COOK TIME: 15 MINS | SKILL LEVEL: 1 (EASY)

INGREDIENTS

200 g jasmine rice
80 ml vegetable oil
2 eggs
1 egg yolk
1 tsp salt
1 tsp sugar
1 tsp chicken stock
  powder
50 g sliced spring onions
30 g butter, melted

METHOD

Wash rice with cold water and drain, repeating three times more. Place drained rice in a rice cooker, add 220 g water and cook according to the manufacturer's instructions. If you don't have a rice cooker, place drained rice in a pot with 220 g water. Bring to the boil over a medium heat, cover and reduce the heat to low. Allow to cook for 25 minutes covered, then remove from the heat and leave to stand for a further 15 minutes, still covered. Fluff grains up with a fork. Leave the rice uncovered in the fridge overnight to dry out.

The next day, heat vegetable oil in a wok, add eggs and yolk and scramble slightly. Before the egg sets, add the rice and stir-fry until the grains separate. Continue stir-frying until the rice is hot, then add the seasonings (salt, pepper and stock powder) and stir through. Add the spring onions and stir-fry until the rawness has been cooked out, then drizzle the butter over and serve.

BARLEY TONIC

SERVINGS: 1 | PREP TIME: 40 MINS PLUS COOLING | COOK TIME: 2 MINS | SKILL LEVEL: 1 (EASY)

INGREDIENTS

Barley water
1 cup pearl barley
1 litre water
5 pieces candied
  winter melon
320 g sugar
  (or more to taste)

1 tall glass
45 ml Australian whisky
  (we used Nant Sherry
  Wood in this recipe)
5 ml (1 tsp) lemon juice
barley water as needed
lemon zest to garnish

METHOD

For the barley water: bring pearl barley, water and candied melon to the boil, and leave to simmer for 30 minutes. Add sugar, stirring until it is all dissolved in the liquid, and simmer for another 10–15 minutes. Allow to cool, and strain before using.

To make the barley tonic: build in a tall glass over ice, topping up with barley water as needed, and garnishing with lemon zest.

TIP

Look for candied winter melon in Asian grocery stores; it's usually found in the snack aisle, next to preserved prunes, toasted seeds and candy.

DARREN ROBERTSON
THREE BLUE DUCKS

**AVOCADO, POACHED EGGS, SOURDOUGH,
FERMENTED WHITE CABBAGE & FENNEL
WITH SOME STUFF FROM THE GARDEN**

You really don't have to wait
until dinner for a great meal.
Great coffee, eggs, butter, avo,
bread, a bit of salad...
a fantastic breakfast can be
just as amazing as anything
consumed after dark.

Darren

BRONTE, NSW

AVOCADO, POACHED EGGS, SOURDOUGH, FERMENTED WHITE CABBAGE & FENNEL WITH SOME STUFF FROM THE GARDEN
AKA AVOCADO TOAST

SERVINGS: 2 | PREP TIME: 10 MINS PLUS KRAUT PREPARATION | SKILL LEVEL: 2 (MODERATE)

INGREDIENTS

Fermented white cabbage and fennel, aka kraut

1 large white cabbage

1 head fennel

2 tbsp salt

4 tsp of your favourite spices, toasted (fennel, coriander, cumin or mustard seeds work a treat)

2 x 900 ml jars, sterilised

a handful of herbs and flowers from the garden – we like…

  fennel fronds

  parsley

  basil

  nasturtiums

  pineapple sage

  chamomile flowers

  baby sorrel

  chives

juice of 1 lime

1 tbsp good-quality olive oil

salt and pepper

4 free-range eggs

1 sourdough bread roll, torn in half

1 clove garlic, halved

1 large, ripe avocado

1 tbsp fermented cabbage and fennel (recipe below)

1 cornichon, chopped

(DF) (V)

METHOD

The kraut recipe will fill a couple of jars, which is of course more than you're going to need for the poached eggs on toast. But if you're going to make your own kraut from scratch, it's well worth making a decent amount!

Remove the dark leaves from the cabbage, then core and shred. Core the fennel and slice it finely. Place the cabbage and fennel in a large bowl, then add the salt. Mix vigorously for 2 minutes and then set aside for 10 minutes to allow the water to leach out. Add the toasted spices, and give it another good mix. Taste the liquid. If it's super-salty, add a little water. If it's too bland, add a little more salt. Halve the mixture into each of the sterilised jars, ensuring there is enough liquid to cover the vegetables. Screw on the lid (not too tightly) and place the jars in a cool, dry place, away from direct sunlight, to ferment. Every 24 hours, gently loosen the lid to allow the gases to escape. Taste the kraut regularly, and once it's reached your preferred level of ferment-y goodness (anywhere from two days to a week), store it in the fridge until needed.

In a bowl, dress the leaves and flowers with a little lime juice, olive oil and salt and pepper to taste. Set aside.

To serve, heat a saucepan full of water to a low simmer. Add a little lime juice and gently crack the eggs in, one at a time. Poach the eggs for about 2 minutes, or until soft-poached. Heat a barbecue or chargrill and place on the bread, torn side down, until toasted. Place the toast on your favourite plate, rub it with the cut side of the garlic and set aside. Peel the avocado, remove the seed and slice the flesh. Season with salt and pepper and place on the toast. Top with some of the fermented vegetables, then two poached eggs, the chopped cornichons and a small pile of dressed herbs and flowers. Drizzle a little extra lime juice and olive oil on top, and a little pinch of salt and pepper.

PHILIP JOHNSON
E'CCO BISTRO

**BANANA TARTE TATIN
WITH RUM & RAISIN
ICE-CREAM**

This dish reminds me of my time in London as a young chef with friends. We made a caramel, threw in Bundy Rum, some bananas, then popped some pastry on top. When it was done we turned it onto a board, topped it with ice cream and ate it straight from the board. Great times!

BRISBANE, QLD

BANANA TARTE TATIN
WITH RUM & RAISIN ICE-CREAM

SERVINGS: 6 | PREP TIME: 40 MINS PLUS SOAKING OVERNIGHT & CHILLING/CHURNING
COOK TIME: 10–12 MINS | SKILL LEVEL: 2 (MODERATE)

INGREDIENTS

Ice-cream
150 g raisins
125 ml (½ cup) dark rum
300 g caster sugar
12 egg yolks
500 ml (2 cups) milk
500 ml (2 cups) cream

Tarte tartin
1 roll frozen butter
  puff pastry, defrosted
  (or use thinly rolled
  home-made pastry)
6 large bananas
250 g caster sugar
60 ml (¼ cup) water
80 ml (⅓ cup) dark rum
60 ml (¼ cup) cream
1 egg, beaten,
  for egg wash

METHOD

For the ice-cream: soak raisins in dark rum overnight.

In a large bowl, whisk together sugar and egg yolks. Place milk and cream in a 2 litre saucepan and bring almost to the boil. Whisk hot milk mixture into the egg mix, then return to a clean saucepan and place over a moderate heat. Using a wooden spoon, stir constantly until custard thickens and coats the back of the spoon. Do not let mixture boil. Strain through a fine sieve, then refrigerate until cold.

Churn cold ice-cream mixture in an ice-cream machine. Once fully churned, stir rum and raisins through, and store in the freezer.

For the tarte tatin: pre-heat the oven to 220°C. Butter a 26–28 cm fry pan. Cut the puff pastry to fit the top of the pan and set aside. Peel bananas and slice thickly on the diagonal.

Combine sugar and water in a small saucepan and stir over a low heat until sugar dissolves. Bring to the boil, and boil without stirring until syrup turns to a dark caramel colour. Immediately remove from the heat and, very carefully, as caramel spits, stir in the rum. Return to a low heat and stir until smooth, then add cream and bring to the boil.

Pour the caramel into the base of the pan. Arrange sliced banana in concentric circles, then top with the puff pastry circle. Egg-wash pastry by brushing with beaten egg. Take care not to let egg run down the edge of the pastry. Bake for 10–12 minutes or until pastry is golden.

To serve: remove the tart from oven and, while still quite hot, invert tart onto the centre of a serving plate. Top each serving with a spoonful of rum and raisin ice-cream.

McLEOD'S SHOOT, NSW

PAM BROOK
BROOKFARM

BUSH SPICE SOUTHERN-STYLE RIBS
CRUNCHY GREEN COLESLAW
CREAMY PARSNIP MASH

I'm not really a recipe-oriented cook. I might get an idea from a recipe but I'll always tweak it depending on what's in the cupboard and how it tastes. We taste everything as we go, adding a little this or a bit of that. It's how you feel on the day that makes the dish special.

Pam

BUSH SPICE SOUTHERN-STYLE RIBS

SERVINGS: 4 | PREP TIME: 10 MINS PLUS MARINATING | COOK TIME: 1½ HOURS | SKILL LEVEL: 1 (EASY)

INGREDIENTS

2 racks pork spare ribs

Dry rub

8 tbsp dark palm sugar or
   dark brown sugar
1 tbsp smoked paprika
1 tsp ground black pepper
1 tsp cayenne powder

1 tsp Cajun spice mix
1 tbsp ground bush tomato
1 tbsp ground pepperberry
1 tsp garlic salt
1 tsp onion powder
1 tsp salt

Liquid

2 cups white wine
4 tbsp white balsamic vinegar
4 tbsp Worcestershire sauce
2 tbsp bush honey
2 cloves garlic, chopped

METHOD

Combine all the ingredients for the dry rub and rub over the ribs. Allow to marinate for 2 hours.

Pre-heat oven to 130°C. Place marinated ribs in a baking pan and pour liquid over. Seal baking pan tightly with tinfoil and bake for 1½ hours.

Pour liquid from pan into a small saucepan; bring to the boil and reduce to a sticky sauce. Pour sauce over ribs and serve with Crunchy Green Coleslaw and Creamy Parsnip Mash.

CRUNCHY GREEN COLESLAW

SERVINGS: 4 | PREP TIME: 15 MINS | SKILL LEVEL: 1 (EASY)

INGREDIENTS

1 small sweetheart cabbage,
   finely sliced (or ordinary
   cabbage if unavailable)
2 cups parsley leaves,
   finely chopped
½ red onion, finely sliced

4 spring onions,
   finely chopped including
   most of the green bits
2 tbsp coarsely
   chopped macadamias

Dressing

⅔ cup plain unsweetened yoghurt
juice of 1 lemon
⅓ cup good-quality macadamia oil
1 tsp sea salt crystals
2 tsp honey (or to taste)

GF V

METHOD

Combine coleslaw ingredients in a bowl and toss well.

Put all dressing ingredients in a jar and shake well until combined. Season to taste with salt and freshly ground black pepper.

Pour dressing over coleslaw just before serving.

CREAMY PARSNIP MASH

SERVINGS: 4 | PREP TIME: 5 MINS | COOK TIME: 15 MINS | SKILL LEVEL: 1 (EASY)

INGREDIENTS

5 parsnips
2 tsp salted butter
½ cup pure cream
2 tsp good-quality
   macadamia oil

GF V

METHOD

Peel parsnips and chop into large cubes. Steam for 15 minutes until soft and easily pierced with a fork.

Place parsnips, butter, cream and macadamia oil in a blender. Blitz until smooth and creamy. Season with salt and pepper to taste.

The Adelaide Central Market is one of the world's great markets. I believe it's because there is an invisible fabric that holds it together. It's about community feeling & bringing people together & people who love food. Every day Adelaide Market brings a new surprise, as the seasons change ... the plums change & the mangoes come in.

Mark.

MARK GLEESON
ADELAIDE CENTRAL MARKET

GLAZED DUCK WITH STAR ANISE,
GINGER & ORANGE
CHICKEN ROLL-UPS

ADELAIDE,
SA

GLAZED DUCK WITH STAR ANISE, GINGER & ORANGE

SERVINGS: 2 | PREP TIME: 15 MINS | COOK TIME: 1¼ HOURS | SKILL LEVEL: 1 (EASY)

INGREDIENTS

2 duck marylands, skin on (look in good poultry stores)

200 g raw sugar

oil for cooking

200 ml chicken stock

grated rind of 1 lemon

2 cups orange juice

6 star anise

50 g fresh ginger, peeled and roughly chopped

4 cloves garlic, roughly chopped

2 bunches (about 200 g) fresh bok choy

METHOD

Pre-heat the oven to 180°C.

Roll the raw duck marylands in the sugar and place in a lightly oiled pan. Bring the pan up to a medium temperature, cooking until the sugar caramelises on the meat. This takes only a few minutes on each side.

Place the duck in a baking dish and add the stock, lemon rind and orange juice. The liquids should cover halfway up the duck – do not completely cover.

Add star anise, ginger, garlic, a pinch of salt and a generous grind of black pepper. Bake for 1¼ hours. Remove duck to a covered pan and keep warm while you finish the sauce. Transfer the sauce to a small saucepan, skim the fat off the top and bring it to the boil. Reduce by one third.

Serve the duck on a bed of washed raw bok choy, with boiling sauce ladled over the meat and greens.

CHICKEN ROLL-UPS

SERVINGS: 4 | PREP TIME: 30 MINS | COOK TIME: 10 MINS | SKILL LEVEL: 1 (EASY)

INGREDIENTS

2 free-range
  chicken breasts

100 ml thick soy sauce

100 ml sweet chilli sauce

juice of 1 lemon

2 carrots

2 Lebanese cucumbers

2 fresh tomatoes

4 roti prata, defrosted
  (packets of 5 are
  available in good Asian
  specialist stores)

100 ml good mayonnaise

100 g dried Asian fried
  onion (available in good
  Asian specialist stores;
  keeps well in the fridge
  after opening)

METHOD

Cut the chicken breasts into long strips 2 cm wide, and marinate for 10 minutes in half the soy sauce, half the chilli sauce and all the lemon juice.

Cut long strips of carrot and cucumber, and chop the tomatoes into small chunks.

Unfold the roti prata, cut each in half and warm in a lightly oiled frying pan. Be careful that they don't dry out as they won't then roll – wrap them in tinfoil after warming to help prevent them drying out.

Barbecue or pan-fry the chicken strips on a low to medium heat for 5–10 minutes, turning occasionally, until they are a golden cooked colour.

Lay a single serve of roti on a chopping board and drizzle with soy sauce, chilli sauce and a little mayonnaise. Place strips of carrot, cucumber and chicken on top and add some chopped tomato. Drizzle with more soy sauce, sprinkle with fried onions and roll the wrap up tightly.

Cut in two, serve and eat immediately – kids will eat these as fast as you can make them!

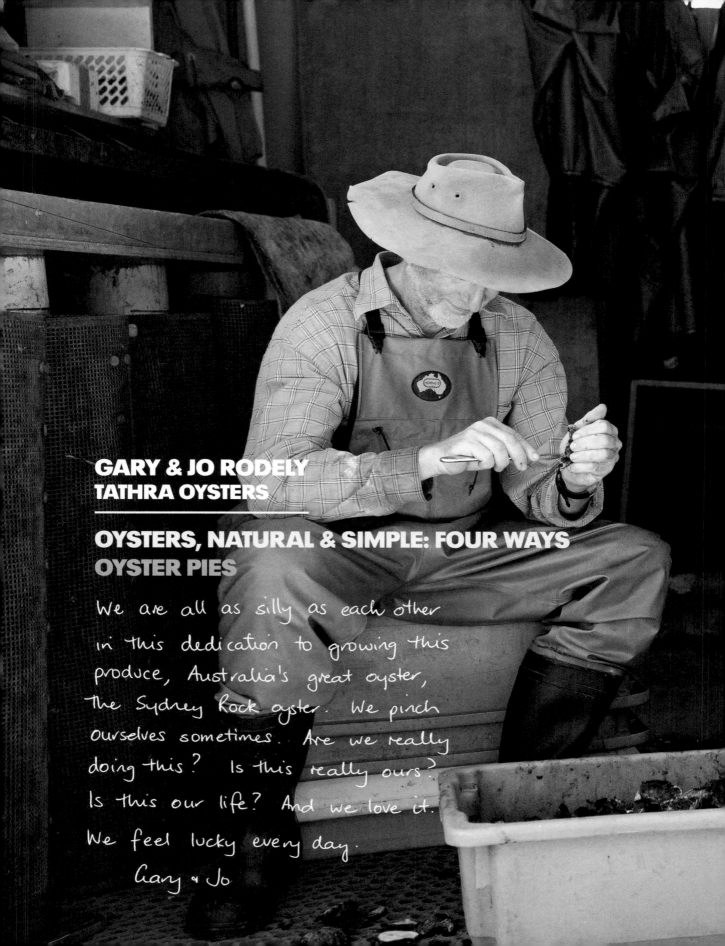

GARY & JO RODELY
TATHRA OYSTERS

OYSTERS, NATURAL & SIMPLE: FOUR WAYS
OYSTER PIES

We are all as silly as each other
in this dedication to growing this
produce, Australia's great oyster,
The Sydney Rock oyster. We pinch
ourselves sometimes. Are we really
doing this? Is this really ours?
Is this our life? And we love it.
We feel lucky every day.
       Gary & Jo

TATHRA,
NSW

OYSTERS, NATURAL & SIMPLE: FOUR WAYS

SERVINGS: 4 | PREP TIME: 10 MINS | SKILL LEVEL: 1 (EASY)

INGREDIENTS

4 dozen (48) plump Sydney Rock Oysters

2 tbsp whole-egg mayonnaise

2 tsp tomato sauce

½ tsp caramelised balsamic vinegar

2 lemons

3 good friends (four people, counting you!)

2 nice bottles of your favourite crisp white wine, chilled

METHOD

Shuck the oysters. For the uninitiated, buy the oysters on the day you plan to eat them and ask your fishmonger to shuck them for you. Plate the shucked oysters on the half shell, cover with plastic wrap and refrigerate.

Remove eight oysters from the fridge 30 minutes before serving. Leave them covered and place them in a cool place, out of direct sunlight.

Immediately prior to serving, remove remaining oysters from the fridge.

In a ramekin, mix together the mayonnaise, tomato sauce and vinegar to your taste.

Plate the oysters onto four plates, placing eight oysters onto each: first two at room temperature, second two still chilled, third two with a small dollop of the sauce and the final two in a bath (not just a few drops) of lemon juice.

Open and serve generous glasses of your favourite white wine.

Taste your way through the different plates. It's amazing the difference these simple things can do to an oyster. Polish off the remaining 16 oysters.

TIP

Not to be confused with their larger, less succulent cousins (Pacific oysters), Sydney Rock Oysters are native and unique to Australia and grow in sheltered estuaries and bays predominantly along the coast of New South Wales.

OYSTER PIES

MAKES: 12 SMALL PIES | PREP TIME: 20 MINS | COOK TIME: 7 MINS | SKILL LEVEL: 1 (EASY)

INGREDIENTS

1 cup small florets of broccoli

90 g butter

½ leek, finely diced

½ cup diced red capsicum

½ cup diced green capsicum

4 tbsp plain flour

300 ml warm milk

½ cup grated cheese

handful of chopped parsley

2 dozen (24) shucked Sydney Rock oysters

3 sheets ready-made shortcrust pastry, defrosted (for pie base)

3 sheets ready-made puff pastry, defrosted (for pie top)

METHOD

Pre-heat pie maker (or oven to 180°C).

Steam broccoli until al dente. Set aside.

Melt butter in a pan and sauté leek and capsicums. Add flour and stir constantly for 1 minute. Gradually add milk, stirring as the sauce thickens. Add cheese, then broccoli. Season to taste with salt and pepper, add parsley and stir. Finally, add oysters to the pan and stir through.

Using the large cutter provided with the pie maker, cut rounds for the bases from the shortcrust pastry and place in the pie maker moulds. Using the smaller cutter, cut rounds for the tops from the puff pastry. Alternatively, line a large pie dish with the shortcrust pastry, line with baking paper and cover the base with ceramic weights or uncooked rice. Bake for 10 minutes then remove the weights (or rice) and paper and bake for a further 5–10 minutes until golden.

Spoon the filling into each pie base (allowing two oysters per small pie) and top with the puff pastry. Seal the lids, crimping the edges with a fork, and cook for 7 minutes until the pastry is golden-brown. If making a large pie in the oven, bake for 30–35 minutes until golden.

Carefully remove each pie from the pie maker or pie dish and allow to cool slightly (the filling will be hot!).

BRIGITTE HAFNER
GERTRUDE STREET ENOTECA

ABRUZZO-STYLE PORK STEW WITH ROASTED CAPSICUM, CHILLI & FENNEL
CHERRY CRUMBLE CAKE

Italian food has been the strongest influence in my cooking life. I was really taken with how Italians approach cooking. How they are obsessive about slicing garlic and how you handle vegetables. They can make zucchini sing in a way I've never seen. Almost all of Italian food is very simple; it's about life and energy, which is how I like to cook.

Brigitte

MORNINGTON
PENINSULA,
VIC

ABRUZZO-STYLE PORK STEW WITH ROASTED CAPSICUM, CHILLI & FENNEL

SERVINGS: 6 | PREP TIME: 45 MINS | COOK TIME: 1–1½ HOURS | SKILL LEVEL: 1 (EASY)

INGREDIENTS

1 kg pork shoulder, cut into 5 cm dice

3 tbsp extra virgin olive oil

70 g fatty pancetta

3 large cloves garlic

½ bunch parsley

1 tsp fennel seeds

⅓ cup medium-bodied white wine

½ tsp dried chilli flakes

1 x 400 g can Italian peeled tomatoes, chopped

2 red capsicums

1 tbsp sherry or red wine vinegar

½ tbsp white sugar

Wet polenta

3 cups water

2 tsp salt

1½ cups fine yellow polenta

1 big knob butter

½ cup grated Parmesan

(GF)

METHOD

In a heavy-based pot such as a cast-iron casserole, brown the pork in the olive oil in small batches. Remove to a plate and sprinkle with salt. Remove the pot from the heat and allow to cool, but don't throw out the fat.

Cut the pancetta into very small pieces, then chop the garlic and parsley as well. Now, combine the pancetta, garlic, parsley and fennel seeds, and using a mezzaluna or a heavy knife, finely chop everything together until you have a fine paste. Add this paste to the pot over a low heat and cook, stirring all the time with a wooden spoon, until the paste becomes fragrant and the garlic turns golden-brown.

Add the pork and its juices back to the pot at once, with the wine and chilli flakes. Increase the heat and simmer for a few minutes, stirring to get the delicious brown stuff off the bottom of the pot and into the sauce. Now add the tomatoes. Reduce the heat to a very low and gentle simmer. Cover with a skewed lid and allow to cook until the pork is tender, about 1–1½ hours.

Pre-heat the oven to 220°C and roast the capsicums until blistered. Cool, peel and chop the flesh into small pieces.

For the wet polenta, bring the water and salt to the boil in a large pot, then add the polenta in a fine, steady stream while stirring with a whisk. Turn the heat to the lowest setting and simmer gently, stirring with a wooden spoon, until very thick (about 15 minutes). Add the butter and Parmesan and serve as soon as possible.

To finish, add the roasted capsicum, sherry or vinegar and sugar to the pork and season with salt if needed. Serve on the wet polenta.

CHERRY CRUMBLE CAKE

MAKES: ONE 20 CM CAKE | PREP TIME: 25 MINS | COOK TIME: 55–60 MINS | SKILL LEVEL: 1 (EASY)

INGREDIENTS

Cake
100 g unsalted butter,
  at room temperature
100 g caster sugar
1 egg
½ tsp vanilla bean paste
125 g self-raising flour, sifted
2 tbsp milk
zest of ½ lemon
250 g pitted cherries, drained

Crumble
90 g plain flour, sifted
50 g light muscovado sugar
½ tsp ground cinnamon
100 g unsalted butter, chilled
25 g rolled oats
20 g ground almonds

METHOD

Pre-heat the oven to 170°C. Butter and line a 20 cm ring tin.

Whip the soft butter and sugar until pale and creamy. Add the egg and vanilla paste and whip until incorporated. Hand-fold in the flour, milk and lemon zest. Spoon into the prepared cake tin and smooth over with a knife.

For the crumble, combine the flour, sugar, cinnamon and butter in a food processor until the mixture just starts to form large clumps. Turn into a bowl and add the oats and ground almonds. Mix together with your hands.

Scatter the cherries over the cake batter and pile the crumble mixture on top. Bake for 55–60 minutes, until a skewer comes out clean when inserted in the middle. Cool on a rack before removing from the tin.

Best eaten on the same day with a dollop of whipped cream.

GEORGE CALOMBARIS

RISOGALO

MELBOURNE, VIC

MY KEY FOOD MANTRA IS NOSTALGIA.
IT'S ABOUT PUTTING SMILES ON PEOPLES
FACES. OUR PAST IS WHAT DETERMINES
OUR FUTURE. WE MUST ALWAYS CELEBRATE
THE PRESENT.

RISOGALO
GEORGE'S RICE PUDDING

SERVINGS: 8 | PREP TIME: 1 HOUR 50 MINS | SKILL LEVEL: 3 (CHALLENGING)

A simplified version of my restaurant's rice pudding. Measurements are in grams as it is more precise when it comes to pastry making.

INGREDIENTS

*Rose-water pastry
(makes approx. 100 pieces)*

125 g butter, at room
   temperature
½ tsp pure vanilla extract,
   or scraped-out seeds of
   1 vanilla bean
90 g sugar
1 egg
250 g standard flour
pinch of salt
½ cup sugar
½ cup water
1 tsp rose-water
250 g icing sugar, sifted

Caramel sauce (makes 200 g)

100 ml cream
100 g sugar
pinch of salt (I use Murray
   River salt)

Rice pudding (makes 2 cups)

50 g risotto rice
500 ml milk
125 ml cream
zest of 1 lemon,
   and 10 ml juice
zest of ½ orange
1 small quill cinnamon
1 whole star anise
1 whole clove
75 g sugar
10 ml lemon juice

To assemble

2 large bananas
large block milk chocolate
   Aero, crushed into pieces
vanilla ice cream, to serve

METHOD

Rose-water pastry: in an electric mixer, cream together the butter, vanilla and sugar until pale. Add the egg and combine. Remove the bowl from the mixer and fold through the flour and salt (it should look like breadcrumbs).

On a floured bench, knead the dough lightly until it forms a ball. Roll the pastry between two sheets of baking paper to a square about 15 cm x 15 cm and 3–5 mm thick. Place on a baking tray lined with baking paper, cover tray with plastic wrap and freeze for 30 minutes. Pre-heat the oven to 180°C fan-forced.

When firm, cut the frozen pastry into small squares, roughly 1 cm x 1 cm (don't worry if they're not completely uniform). Bake the squares for 10 minutes fan-forced, or until golden-brown.

Meanwhile, heat the sugar and water in a small saucepan over a medium heat until the sugar is dissolved. Remove from the heat and stir the rose-water into the syrup until combined. Remove the hot pastry squares from the oven, quickly dip them into the rose-water syrup and drain on a wire rack. Once cool, dust the squares with icing sugar and store in an airtight container until needed.

Caramel sauce: while the pastry is in the freezer, make the caramel sauce. Gently heat the cream in a small saucepan; set aside. Heat the sugar in a medium-sized, heavy-based, non-stick frying pan over a low to medium heat. Do not stir the sugar. Allow it to melt completely and turn amber in colour, being careful not to let it burn. This should take 8–12 minutes.

Stir the heated cream into the melted sugar until combined. Allow the caramel mixture to boil for 1 minute. Then add the salt, remove the pan from the heat, stir briefly and allow the caramel to rest for 10 minutes until cooled slightly. Strain the sauce through a mesh sieve and cool completely before serving.

Rice pudding: place the rice, milk, cream, half the lemon zest, all the orange zest, and the spices in a medium-sized, heavy-based saucepan over a medium heat and bring to the boil, stirring occasionally. Reduce the heat to low and add the sugar. Cook, stirring constantly, until one-third of the liquid has evaporated and the mixture has begun to thicken slightly. This should take approximately 30–40 minutes. Remove the rice pudding from the heat when the rice is soft and the sauce looks like custard. Remove the spices and stir in the remaining lemon zest and the lemon juice, until combined. Set aside until ready to serve.

To assemble: into 8 ramekins or similar (½ cup capacity), spoon 2–4 tablespoons of warm rice pudding. Top each with 1–2 tablespoons caramel sauce, ¼ banana cut into thin slices, a few cubes of rose-water pastry and a sprinkling of crushed Aero pieces. Serve with vanilla ice cream.

ROSS & JANE FARGHER
PRAIRIE HOTEL

SLOW-COOKED HARISSA GOAT
STOCKMAN'S ROAST LAMB FRITTERS

25 years ago, Ross + I bought our local pub +
who would have guessed it would become
the adventure it has been, + continues
to be. Our family has been in the area for
well over 150 years + our relationship with
the land has given us the resilience to
stay. It's the sort of place you always
come back to ~ that you never get out
of your blood.
                                    Jane

PARACHILNA,
SA

SLOW-COOKED HARISSA GOAT

SERVINGS: 4–6 | PREP TIME: 15 MINS | COOK TIME: 1½–2 HOURS | SKILL LEVEL: 1 (EASY)

INGREDIENTS

Harissa
300 g roasted capsicum
1 red onion
75 g brown sugar
juice of 1 lemon
4 cloves garlic
2 fresh red chillies
1 bunch coriander
½ bunch mint
2 tbsp paprika
2 tbsp ground coriander
200 ml red wine vinegar
300 ml olive oil

1–1.5 kg diced goat (your butcher
  should be able to order it for you)
a little oil for browning
zest of 1 lemon
4 bay leaves
1 x 420 g can diced tomatoes
2 brown onions,
  sliced and sautéed until soft

METHOD

Pre-heat oven to 160°C.

Blend all harissa ingredients in a food processor until smooth, adding salt and pepper to taste.

Season diced goat with salt and pepper. Seal and brown in a frying pan – remove to a large bowl to cool, retaining the liquid from the pan if any.

Combine browned goat, pan juices, lemon zest, bay leaves, diced tomatoes, sautéed onion and two-thirds of the harissa. Mix together thoroughly. Put into a braising pan or similar. Cover and place in heated oven for approximately 1½–2 hours, or until meat is tender.

When serving stir in the remaining harissa. Serve with either rice or couscous. Enjoy.

STOCKMAN'S ROAST LAMB FRITTERS

MAKES: 8–10 | PREP TIME: 15 MINS PLUS RESTING | COOK TIME: 5 MINS | SKILL LEVEL: 1 (EASY)

INGREDIENTS

2 cups self-raising flour

1 x 330 ml can of beer at room temperature (½ can for the fritters; the other ½ for the cook)

1 cup warmed milk (approx.)

2 cups trimmed and diced cold cooked lamb (preferably left over from last night's roast dinner)

dripping (best saved from roasting pan) – can be substituted with cooking oil

favourite tomato sauce for dunking

METHOD

Season flour with salt and pepper and place in a mixing bowl. Make a well in the centre – pour in beer and slowly fold in flour, adding sufficient milk to create a batter of a thick consistency. Add meat and combine. Rest mixture for about 30 minutes.

Heat dripping or oil (approximately depth 15–20 mm) in a large frying pan. Add a small drop of batter to test the temperature – the batter should sizzle.

Once the correct temperature has been established, carefully drop heaped tablespoons of fritter mix into the pan. Cook until golden-brown (1–2 minutes) before turning over. Once cooked on both sides, remove fritters and drain off excess dripping/oil on a rack or paper towel. Keep warm in oven while the rest of the fritters are being cooked.

Best enjoyed with tomato sauce or similar.

REDFERN,
NSW

AUNTY BERYL VAN-OPLOO

CHARGRILLED KANGAROO FILLET WITH SWEET POTATO MASH, QUANDONG JUS & WARRIGAL GREENS

I'm proud to come from a people that have thrived by passing traditions and knowledge on to each new generation. Talking about our food is an important way of keeping our culture alive. It makes me happy to see people integrating it into their own cultures too. Kangaroo curry? Now that's Australian.

Aunty Beryl.

CHARGRILLED KANGAROO FILLET
WITH SWEET POTATO MASH, QUANDONG JUS
& WARRIGAL GREENS

SERVINGS: 4 | PREP TIME: 30 MINS | COOK TIME: 45 MINS | SKILL LEVEL: 1 (EASY)

INGREDIENTS

Sweet potato mash
2 large sweet potatoes
1 tbsp unsalted butter
salt and pepper

Kangaroo
4 x 180–200 g
  kangaroo fillets
salt and pepper
olive oil

Quandong jus
1¼ cups kangaroo
  or game stock
¼ cup port
2 tbsp quandong jam
salt and pepper

Warrigal greens
5 cups warrigal greens
  (English spinach works
  well if you can't get them)

METHOD

Pre-heat the oven to 160°C and then wrap the sweet potatoes in tinfoil and bake them for 45 minutes, or until soft. Remove the potatoes from the tinfoil and scoop the flesh from the skins into a mixing bowl. Using a fork, mash the sweet potatoes with the butter and season to taste. For a smoother consistency, push the mash through a sieve. Set aside and keep warm.

To prepare the kangaroo fillets: season and lightly brush with olive oil. On a hot barbecue or chargrill, cook the fillets for about 4 minutes on each side for a medium-rare steak and set aside for 10 minutes, wrapped in tinfoil, to rest.

To make the jus: in a saucepan on a medium to high heat, reduce the stock by half, then add the port and the quandong jam. Stir to combine and bring the sauce to a simmer. Season to taste and reduce further if desired. Set aside and keep warm.

To cook the warrigal greens: bring 2 litres of water and a good pinch of salt to the boil in a large saucepan. Carefully lower in the greens and blanch for 30 seconds. Immediately strain and refresh under cold water. Drain and set aside.

To assemble: slice the rested kangaroo fillets to your desired thickness. On a serving plate, place a large spoonful of mash in the centre, then place the greens on top, followed by the sliced fillets. Drizzle the lot with the resting juices and quandong jus, and finish with a little olive oil and a little salt and pepper to taste.

DANIEL WILSON
HUXTABLE

SAUSAGE ROLLS WITH TOMATO RELISH

DARK CHOCOLATE & RASPBERRY CUPCAKES WITH RASPBERRY BUTTERCREAM ICING

Eating food is about making memories.
And going to friends' birthday parties
as a kid was that for me. I loved
putting Cheezels on my fingers &
eating sausage rolls. Birthday parties
are different adventures now, but
nothing's changed; great food is still
the centre of every celebration.
We did these recipes for Grace's 9th
birthday party – a Grumpy Cat & onesie
sleepover!

Daniel

NORTH MELBOURNE,
VIC

SAUSAGE ROLLS WITH TOMATO RELISH

MAKES: ABOUT 50 | PREP TIME: 1 HOUR PLUS FREEZING
COOK TIME: 20 MINS | SKILL LEVEL: 2 (MODERATE)

INGREDIENTS

400 g beef mince
200 g veal mince
200 g pork mince
1 medium carrot, minced
½ stick celery, minced
1 brown onion, minced
¼ cup finely
  chopped parsley
2 cloves garlic, minced
2 tbsp potato starch
  (available at Asian
  grocery stores)
8 sheets butter puff pastry
4 egg yolks,
  mixed with a fork

Tomato relish
4 ripe tomatoes, diced
2 brown onions, diced
6 cloves garlic, sliced
½ cup raw sugar
½ cup malt vinegar
½ cup water
1 stick cinnamon
2 star anise

METHOD

For the sausage mix: place all three meats in a food processor and pulse until almost fine, but with some texture still. Place in a large bowl and add the vegetables, parsley, garlic, potato starch, and salt and pepper to taste. Mix well, until the sausage mix is emulsified. You can do this by beating it against the sides of the bowl. You must make sure that it remains as cold as possible at all times, otherwise it can split. Reserve, covered, in the fridge until needed.

To make the sausage rolls: place a sheet of puff pastry on your chopping board and cut it in half lengthways. Try to work quickly so that the pastry doesn't get too warm and soft. Roll enough of the sausage mix into a 2 cm thick log to fit the length of the pastry. Place on the pastry, about a third of the way back from one edge. Using a pastry brush, place some egg yolk on the wide part of the pastry. Fold over the narrow part of the pastry and stick it down on the part with the egg. Try to make sure that the pastry is snug around the sausage, then press the two layers of pastry together with a fork all the way along the joined pastry. Place on a lined tray in the freezer to firm up (freezing the sausage rolls makes them much easier to cut, and also the pastry cooks better from frozen). Repeat with the rest of the pastry and sausage mix.

For the relish: cook everything down together until thick. Remove spices, and blitz in a food processor.

To cook the sausage rolls: pre-heat the oven to 200°C. Remove the sausage roll logs from the freezer, brush the tops with egg yolk and allow them to sit for 10–15 minutes to soften slightly. Slice into about 8 pieces per log, or whatever size you like. Place on a lined tray, without overcrowding them. Place in the oven for 20 minutes. The sausage rolls should be golden and the pastry crisp. Allow to sit for 5 minutes before serving, as they will be very hot!

Alternative 'grown-up' version: dice 150 g sharp cheddar and 3 tablespoons of pickled jalapeños and mix into the sausage mix!

DARK CHOCOLATE & RASPBERRY CUPCAKES WITH RASPBERRY BUTTERCREAM ICING

MAKES: 24 | PREP TIME: 40 MINS | COOK TIME: 20 MINS | SKILL LEVEL: 1 (EASY)

INGREDIENTS

120 g butter
½ cup vegetable oil
1 cup water
100 g dark chocolate
 (70% cocoa)
1½ cups caster sugar
½ cup cocoa, sifted
2 eggs
seeds of ½ vanilla bean
1½ tsp baking powder
1 tsp baking soda
1 cup milk
juice of 1 lemon
2 cups flour
1 cup raspberries

Raspberry buttercream

1 cup frozen raspberries
1½ cups icing sugar
zest and juice of 1 lemon
200 g unsalted butter,
 diced and softened
seeds of ½ vanilla bean

METHOD

Pre-heat oven to 180°C. Line two 12-hole muffin trays with patty-pan cases.

Place butter, oil, water and chocolate in a glass or stainless-steel bowl, and place over a pot of simmering water to melt. Remove the bowl from the pot and stir to combine. Whisk in the sugar and cocoa, making sure the mixture is well combined with no lumps. Whisk in eggs and vanilla seeds.

Mix baking powder and baking soda into milk, then add lemon juice. Mix into chocolate mixture along with flour, whisking until evenly combined to a smooth batter. Spoon mixture into paper cases, up to about three-quarters full. Push 2–3 raspberries into each.

Bake cupcakes for about 20 minutes or until an inserted skewer comes out clean. Stand for 5 minutes to set before removing from the pan. Leave to cool before icing.

To make the buttercream, place raspberries in a small pot with ½ cup of icing sugar over a low heat, and stir to dissolve. Add lemon juice and cook for 5 minutes or until the fruit is all broken down. Purée with a stick blender and pass through a fine sieve. Place in the fridge to cool down.

Place butter, lemon zest and remaining icing sugar in the mixing bowl of an upright mixer with a whisk attachment, and whip while slowly adding the raspberry sauce until well combined.

Scoop the buttercream into a piping bag with a star tip and pipe onto the cupcakes once they are cold.

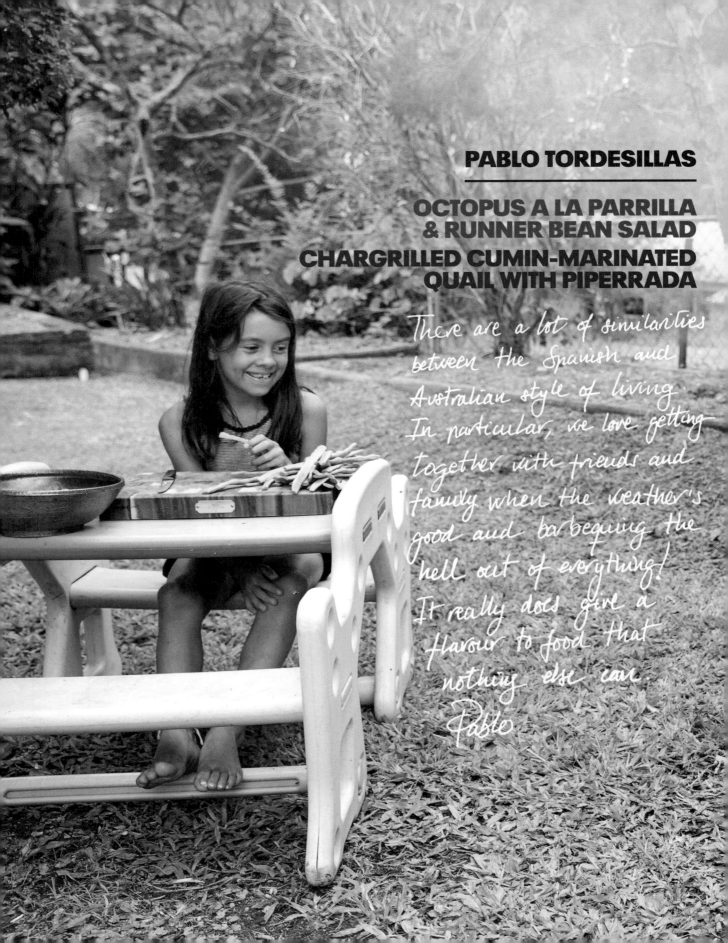

PABLO TORDESILLAS

OCTOPUS A LA PARRILLA & RUNNER BEAN SALAD
CHARGRILLED CUMIN-MARINATED QUAIL WITH PIPERRADA

There are a lot of similarities between the Spanish and Australian style of living. In particular, we love getting together with friends and family when the weather's good and barbequing the hell out of everything! It really does give a flavour to food that nothing else can.

Pablo

COORPAROO
QLD

OCTOPUS A LA PARRILLA & RUNNER BEAN SALAD
BARBECUED OCTOPUS SALAD

SERVINGS: 6 | PREP & COOK TIME: 1¼ HOURS | SKILL LEVEL: 1 (EASY)

INGREDIENTS

100 g salt

1 bay leaf

1 wine cork (required by tradition!)

1 kg octopus, cleaned

3 large bulb spring onions

2 cloves garlic, peeled

750 g runner beans

⅓ bunch flat-leaf parsley

400 g Kipfler potatoes

1 tbsp sweet Spanish paprika (pimentón)

150 g black olives

lemon juice to taste

140 ml extra virgin olive oil

METHOD

Start your coals or wood fire (you could also use a gas barbecue).

Three-quarters fill a large pot with water and add salt, bay leaf and wine cork. Bring to the boil and dip the octopus in for about 10 seconds to set its gelatine. Bring the water back up to the boil and re-dip the octopus. Repeat twice more, leaving the octopus in the last time. Turn the heat down and simmer for 40–45 minutes. Use a skewer to check the top part of the tentacles – if it's ready, the skewer should go through without much resistance. Leave to cool in the cooking liquor.

In the meantime, prepare your ingredients. Finely chop the spring onions and garlic. Top and tail the runner beans and cut at an angle into short lengths. Wash the parsley and chop roughly. Wash the potatoes, boil for 6–8 minutes depending on size, and cut into 5 mm rounds. If you wish, you can use the octopus liquid for cooking the potatoes.

Heat 100 ml of the olive oil in a medium-sized, heavy-based pan over a low flame, then add the onion and garlic and sweat gently for about 20 minutes, stirring occasionally to avoid browning. Once they're soft, remove from the heat and add the paprika. Keep stirring so it doesn't burn.

Blanch the runner beans in salted boiling water, then drain and, while they're still hot, incorporate with the onion and garlic mixture along with the potatoes and black olives. The residual heat from the beans will help to blend all the ingredients together.

Once the coals are ready, chargrill the octopus until the ends of the tentacles are charred, crisp and smoky; this takes about 3–4 minutes each side. Cut the octopus into chunks, keeping the tentacle ends in one piece, and toss into the bean mixture. Adjust seasoning with salt and pepper, dress with lemon juice and remaining olive oil, sprinkle the parsley over and mix lightly.

CHARGRILLED CUMIN-MARINATED QUAIL WITH PIPERRADA

SERVINGS: 4 | PREP & COOK TIME: 1¼ HOURS PLUS MARINATING | SKILL LEVEL: 1 (EASY)

Piperrada is a typical Basque side dish made with tomatoes, capsicums and onions.

INGREDIENTS

4 quail, butterflied

2 large red capsicums

2 large green capsicums

200 g pimientos del piquillo (piquillo peppers; optional)

4 ripe tomatoes

4 large cloves garlic, peeled

½ bunch chives

200 ml extra virgin olive oil

100 ml (approx.) sherry vinegar

Spice mix

50 g cumin seeds

25 g coriander seeds

12 g black peppercorns

 DF GF

METHOD

To make the spice mix: lightly roast, grind and sieve the cumin and coriander seeds and black peppercorns. Rub this spice mix all over the quail a few hours prior to cooking.

For the piperrada: heat coals (or a gas barbecue if you don't have coals) and roast the red and green capsicums for about 10 minutes, turning every couple of minutes. Allow to cool a little, then peel, de-seed and cut into thin strips. Keep the coals hot for cooking the quail later.

Cut the pimientos, if using, into thin strips. Peel, de-seed and finely chop the tomatoes. Finely chop the garlic and chives.

Heat a good amount of olive oil in a wide, heavy-based pan over a medium flame, then add the garlic and sweat until lightly brown and nutty. Incorporate the tomato and cook for 15 minutes. Turn the heat down, then add the capsicums and pimientos (if using), and cook for another 15 minutes. Turn the heat off and pour in sherry vinegar to taste. The piperrada should be slightly sharp.

Sprinkle the chopped chives over just before serving.

Salt your quail and lay them on a parrilla (grill) over the coals where you roasted the capsicums. Grill each side until crisp and smoky, avoiding overcooking them.

Rest quail for 15 minutes, then serve with the piperrada and a crusty baguette to mop up the juices.

Food should turn on your taste buds
and it should never be taken too seriously!
I like food that is a little irreverent,
a bit whimsical, a bit pop art.
All these elements play out in my head
when I put dishes together.
It's about seduction – you should want
to just dive right in.

Christine

ELIZABETH BAY,
NSW

CHRISTINE MANFIELD

TAMARIND PRAWNS & EGGPLANT
PASSIONFRUIT & MANGO SUNDAE

TAMARIND PRAWNS & EGGPLANT

SERVINGS: 4 | PREP TIME: 20 MINS | COOK TIME: 15 MINS | SKILL LEVEL: 2 (MODERATE)

INGREDIENTS

16 cherry tomatoes

1.3 litres oil for deep-frying

2 tbsp curry leaves

1 eggplant (300 g)

400 g raw king prawn
    tail meat

1 tsp turmeric

1 tsp Kashmiri chilli powder

2 tsp roasted
    ground coriander

1 tsp salt

2 tbsp sunflower oil

4 tbsp chopped
    coriander leaves

Tamarind sauce

150 g tamarind pulp

300 ml water

2 tbsp sunflower oil

1 tsp brown mustard seeds

1 tsp fenugreek seeds

6 red shallots, finely diced

12 curry leaves

2 small green chillies,
    minced

1 tbsp ginger and
    garlic paste

2 ripe tomatoes,
    de-seeded and chopped

1 tsp Kashmiri chilli powder

½ tsp turmeric

1 tsp roasted ground
    coriander

1 tsp sea salt flakes

METHOD

Pre-heat oven to 160°C. Cut tomatoes in half and roast in oven for 15 minutes. Set aside.

Heat 300 ml of the oil to 160°C in a small saucepan. Add curry leaves (they will sputter) and fry for 10 seconds. Remove with a mesh spoon and drain on a paper towel. Set aside.

Heat remaining oil to 180°C in a deep-fryer or deep saucepan. Cut eggplant into chunks and deep-fry until golden. Set aside.

De-vein and butterfly the prawn tails. Pat dry. Mix turmeric, chilli powder, ground coriander and salt with just enough water to make a paste. Stir prawns into the paste and toss to coat. Set aside while you prepare the sauce.

Tamarind sauce: break tamarind pulp into pieces and place in a small saucepan with water. Bring to the boil, remove from the heat and leave for 10 minutes, then further break up tamarind in the water with your fingers. Press through a chinois sieve to extract tamarind liquid; discard solids.

Heat oil in a frying pan over a medium heat and add mustard seeds. When they start to pop, add fenugreek seeds and fry for a few seconds, being careful not to burn them (if you burn them, they become bitter).

Add shallots, curry leaves and green chilli and cook over a moderate heat for about 2 minutes, until softened but not coloured.

Stir in ginger and garlic paste and sauté for 1 minute, then add tomato and cook for 2 minutes until softened.

Add spices, salt and tamarind liquid and bring to simmering point. Simmer the sauce until it thickens, about 5 minutes.

To cook the prawns, heat sunflower oil in a frying pan and fry prawns over a high heat for 2 minutes until just cooked and starting to colour, then add prawns to the sauce along with the roasted cherry tomatoes and fried eggplant, and stir to combine. Cook for 1 minute only, then remove from heat and stir through the chopped coriander. Scatter with fried curry leaves and serve.

PASSIONFRUIT & MANGO SUNDAE

SERVINGS: 4 | PREP TIME: 1¼ HOURS PLUS COOLING AND CHURNING
COOK TIME: 45 MINUTES | SKILL LEVEL: 2 (MODERATE)

INGREDIENTS

Passionfruit curd

3 large egg yolks

60 g caster sugar

65 ml strained fresh
  passionfruit juice

75 g cold, unsalted butter,
  cut into cubes

Passionfruit ice-cream

100 g caster sugar

3 large egg yolks

250 ml pouring
  (35% fat) cream

125 ml passionfruit juice

Meringue shards

60 g egg whites

120 g caster sugar

pinch sea salt flakes

Coconut clouds

25 g caster sugar

½ pinch sea salt flakes

250 ml coconut cream

Caramel popcorn

2 tsp vegetable oil

40 g popping corn

120 g caster sugar

2 tsp butter

To assemble

1 large mango,
  sliced or diced

4 passionfruit, pulp only

4 fresh lychees, halved
  (can also use rambutans
  or longans)

16 small mint leaves

1 tsp freeze-dried
  mint powder (optional),
  for dusting

METHOD

Passionfruit curd: whisk egg yolks and sugar in a heatproof bowl until light and fluffy. Add passionfruit juice, then stand the bowl over a pan of simmering water and cook until thick, stirring constantly.

Add butter, piece by piece, allowing each piece to incorporate before stirring in the next. The mixture should have become thicker by the time the last piece of butter has been added. Remove bowl from the heat and place it on ice to cool.

Cover the surface with plastic wrap to seal. Store curd in a sealed container in the fridge.

Passionfruit ice-cream: whisk sugar and egg yolks in a heatproof bowl until pale and creamy.

Bring half the cream to simmering point in a saucepan.

Whisk passionfruit juice into the egg mixture, then slowly whisk in the hot cream.

Stand the bowl over a pan of simmering water and cook gently, stirring, until the mixture coats the back of a spoon.

Pass the custard through a fine-meshed sieve into another bowl, then whisk in remaining cream and allow to cool. Churn cooled passionfruit mixture in an ice-cream machine, then store in the freezer until ready to serve.

Meringue shards: Pre-heat oven to 70°C. Whisk egg whites to soft peaks in a food processor on medium speed, then slowly add sugar and salt with the motor running. Whisk to stiff peaks that are firm and glossy, about 4 minutes.

With a large palette knife, spread egg mixture onto two baking trays lined with baking paper or non-stick mats to make a thin layer, 3 mm thick. Bake for 45 minutes until dry and crisp.

Allow to cool, then break into free-form shards. Store in an airtight container between sheets of baking paper, until ready to serve.

Coconut clouds: stir sugar and salt into coconut cream. Pour into a siphon canister and shake to combine. Store in fridge until ready to use. When ready, aerate in canister with two cream chargers, shaking after each charge. (If you don't have a siphon canister, you can substitute the clouds with a few blobs of coconut gelato or sorbet.)

Caramel popcorn: heat oil in a lidded saucepan over a medium heat and add the popping corn. Quickly cover with lid and shake pan gently until the corn becomes popcorn. Remove from heat and pour into a bowl, discarding any hard pieces.

Heat sugar and 40 ml water in a saucepan until sugar melts and darkens to a caramel, swirling the pan rather than stirring. When it becomes caramel, add butter and swirl to combine.

Pour popcorn into caramel and toss through to coat evenly. Pour onto a flat tray lined with baking paper or a non-stick mat and leave to cool and harden.

To assemble, spoon passionfruit curd onto centre of each serving bowl or glass. Arrange mango, passionfruit pulp and lychees on top, and scatter a few tiny mint leaves around the fruit. Use a scoop to make a ball of passionfruit ice-cream, and sit this on top of the fruit. Scatter the meringue shards, coconut clouds, caramel popcorn and sprinkles of mint powder (if using) randomly over the dessert.

LEANNE GRAY
SILO BAKERY + CAFE

MUM'S WELSH PASTY
TARTE FLAMICHE

I arrive at the shop as the restaurants
in our street are closing and it's dark
and quiet. There's something lonely
about the constant rhythmic whir of
the dough hook in the machine.
And after 18 years in this spot, I still
love filling up these glass cabinets with
these pastries.

KINGSTON,
ACT

MUM'S WELSH PASTY

MAKES: 10 | PREP TIME: 25 MINS | COOK TIME: 45 MINS | SKILL LEVEL: 2 (MODERATE)

INGREDIENTS

500 g plain flour
120 g mashed potato
120g butter or lard, diced
good pinch of salt
2 tsp baking powder
cold water to mix
  (approx. 150 ml)
250 g lamb mince
300 g diced swede
300 g diced carrot
500 g diced potato
½ small onion, diced
2 tsp salt flakes
2 tsp ground black pepper
1 egg, beaten

METHOD

Pre-heat oven to 200°C.

Combine flour, mashed potato, butter or lard, salt and baking powder. Add water and gently mix or knead until the dough comes together. Roll to desired thickness and cut into 18 cm rounds.

Combine meat, vegetables and seasoning, and mix well so that the lamb mince binds the vegetables.

Brush edges of pastry rounds with beaten egg. Portion the meat and vegetable filling onto half of each pastry round, fold over the pastry to enclose the filling, seal, crimp the edges with your hands and paint top of pasties with remaining egg wash. Place on baking trays and bake for 45 minutes. Serve hot.

TARTE FLAMICHE
FLEMISH LEEK & CHEESE PASTRY

SERVINGS: 6 | PREP TIME: 30 MINS PLUS CHILLING | COOK TIME: 25 MINS | SKILL LEVEL: 1 (EASY)

INGREDIENTS

600 g good-quality
  puff pastry
3 leeks, cleaned and
  cut into 8 cm lengths
fresh thyme leaves
  from 1 sprig
250 g sour cream
  or mascarpone
300 g washed-rind cheese
  (such as Jensen's Red,
  Époisses de Bourgogne,
  Munster)

(V)

METHOD

Roll pastry to approximately ¼ cm thick and cut into approximately 6 rectangles about 14 cm x 8 cm in size. Chill for about an hour.

Place leek sections into a little water in a saucepan, along with thyme. Bring to the boil and simmer for 10 minutes or so, until soft. Season with salt and pepper. Chill for another hour.

Pre-heat the oven to 200°C.

To assemble the tartes, place a spoonful of sour cream or mascarpone in the centre of each pastry rectangle. Place one piece of leek on top, then a slice of cheese (the rind can be removed for a milder version). Fold in the narrow ends of the pastry to the centre, as if it were an envelope. The leek and cheese should be cradled in the middle of the tarte. Bake for 25 minutes. Serve hot.

PETER RUSSELL-CLARKE

MANGO & FIG OMELETTE
PETER'S SMOKED TROUT SOUP

G'day

As a painter I'm concerned with colour, form,
texture & shape. And as a cook I'm concerned
with exactly the same things.

How textures & colours are put together on a plate
or on a canvas is important. We do it so people
say "I appreciate what you've done & I'm enjoying
myself by looking at it — or eating it — or
savouring its colours & textures."

Peter

TOOBORAC,
VIC

MANGO & FIG OMELETTE

SERVINGS: 1 | PREP TIME: 10 MINS | SKILL LEVEL: 1 (EASY)

INGREDIENTS

1 tsp finely minced ginger (the processed bottled product is OK)

a splash of extra virgin olive oil

butter – proper butter, not pretend butter!

2 eggs per omelette (in my humble opinion, 3 is just too many – your omelette becomes a full meal whereas it's my intention to serve a light entrée – so, 2 eggs)

garlic salt

a reasonable amount of chopped spring onion

the cheek of a mango with its skin off

a fig halved or quartered so you see the glorious design of its interior

slice of smoked salmon

METHOD

In a small pan (20 cm diameter), dollop the ginger, olive oil and a generous dessertspoon of butter. Melt the butter and break the eggs into the pan.

Stir the eggs, not too vigorously, then let them set on the bottom. (I often turn off the gas so that this process is done gently.)

Sprinkle a little garlic salt on the eggs, which will be just starting to firm. Also add the chopped spring onion (just a few flicks will do). Now lay the mango cheek on the side of the omelette that's away from the pan's handle, and place the fig pieces each side of it.

The top of the omelette will have firmed by now, as you will have turned on the heat again. Tilt the pan so that any 'wet' egg runs down the side of the omelette and firms. (You'll notice that the melted butter and oil will make the top of the omelette wet. That's good.)

Take the pan to the table and, folding the handle-end of the omelette over the other half of the omelette, slide it folded onto the plate. Place a slice of smoked salmon beside the folded creation and wait for the applause.

Do not drink alcohol during this manoeuvre, as one will become befuddled.

TIP

If mangoes and figs aren't in season, I've used strawberries, oranges, even a dollop of marmalade jam to which I've added chilli and garlic. In fact, whatever flavours or textures you like most and are in season or available can only enhance your end product – the omelette.

PETER'S SMOKED TROUT SOUP

SERVINGS: 4 | PREP TIME: ½–1 HOUR | SKILL LEVEL: 1 (EASY)

INGREDIENTS

obtain 1 or 2 good
    smoked trout
3–4 cups good beef stock
handful of small
    spinach leaves

METHOD

Skin trout and de-bone them. Put everything – heads, tails, skin, etc. – except the marvellous flesh into an appropriately sized pot with the beef stock. I don't use fish stock, as I want the full flavour of the beef. I also don't add salt as, if one is using commercially made stock then it's got plenty of salt in it or, if you've made your own stock, no doubt you will have used salt in its creation.

Boil the lot for enough time for the flavour to be boiled out from the skin and bones, and serve the clear liquid with a little of the flesh you'd put aside, plus a couple of small spinach leaves. Do not be tempted to add cream or, indeed, anything else.

Do not add salt, but include a bottle of pinot grigio on the table.

TIP

The remaining trout flesh can be served, either alongside the soup or separately another time, on raw spinach leaves sprinkled judiciously with shaved Parmesan and decorated with a circle of peeled orange. I then splash a little mirin over the lot and serve. Crisp iceberg lettuce is a good substitute for spinach, and either sweet sherry or lemon juice instead of mirin.

Most Sundays, my grandson, Teddy, comes to my house and we cook roast Chicken and vegetarian fried rice. In my younger days we had no Sundays off — every day was a restaurant day. Now, I have a little bit more time and I like spending it with my family, cooking and, of course, eating.

Gilbert.

GILBERT LAU AM

LAU'S FAMILY ROAST CHICKEN
TEDDY'S VEGETARIAN FRIED RICE

BRIGHTON,
VIC

LAU'S FAMILY ROAST CHICKEN

SERVINGS: 4 | PREP TIME: 15 MINS | COOK TIME: 65 MINS | SKILL LEVEL: 1 (EASY)

INGREDIENTS

1.5 kg free-range chicken (no bigger), washed and dried thoroughly inside and out

olive oil for coating the skin

For cavity
thumb-sized piece of ginger, grated

½ tsp sea salt

½ tsp brown sugar

few drops sesame oil

2 spring onions, trimmed, washed and folded into three

¾ tbsp light soy sauce

2 cloves garlic, skin on and lightly smashed

2–3 tbsp Shaoxing wine (not salty cooking Shaoxing wine)

1–2 grinds white pepper

For sauce
¼ cup water

½ tsp potato flour

METHOD

Pre-heat oven to 185°C.

Combine the cavity ingredients in a bowl and place in chicken cavity. Close the back of the chicken with a skewer, making sure to gather in all the loose skin so the moisture stays in.

Rub chicken skin with olive oil and sea salt, and put chicken on a rack placed in a roasting dish containing ½ cup of water. Roast for 65 minutes, then remove from oven and drain any cavity juices into the roasting pan. Cover chicken and rest for 5 minutes.

For the sauce, combine water and potato flour. Skim any fat from the juices in the pan, and deglaze (stir to mix in any flavours stuck to the bottom of the pan). Add water and potato flour mixture and stir over a low heat until thickened. Strain.

Serve chicken with sauce and Teddy's Vegetarian Fried Rice.

TEDDY'S VEGETARIAN FRIED RICE

SERVINGS: 4 | PREP TIME: 40 MINS | SKILL LEVEL: 1 (EASY)

INGREDIENTS

2½ tbsp light olive oil or sunflower oil (add extra if needed)

2 eggs, lightly beaten

30 g shelled sugar peas

10–12 sugar pea pods, string removed, washed and finely chopped

60 g small to medium Swiss brown mushrooms, thinly sliced

⅓ teaspoon peeled and finely diced ginger

35 g freshly cooked sweetcorn kernels

400 g steamed rice

½ tsp sea salt

2 young spring onions, outer layer removed and finely chopped

1 tbsp light soy sauce

METHOD

Place a large wok over a medium heat and add 1½ tablespoons of oil. When oil is shimmering, add eggs and quickly stir until beginning to firm, then remove from wok and set aside.

Add ½ tablespoon of oil and remaining ingredients, except the spring onions and soy sauce. Stir for 30 seconds, breaking up the rice. Return egg to wok and add soy sauce and remaining oil, and combine. When hot enough, stir spring onions through and serve.

INDEX

 = **DAIRY FREE**   = **GLUTEN FREE**   V = **VEGETARIAN**

Page numbers in italics refer to photographs.

VEGETARIAN

CONTRIBUTORS

ACKNOWLEDGEMENTS

We are profoundly grateful to everyone who contributed to the making of *The Great Australian Cookbook*. We would especially like to thank: the 4Fourteen team; the staff at The Adge Apartment Hotel; David Albert; Patricia Amad; Mario Ascensio; Jules Bagnato; Marianne Baker; Kylie Ball; Katie Barnett; Mette Bassham; Colin Beer; the team at Berardo's; Mindy Bonomelli and Rohan McGlew; Samuel Brading; the Brook family; James Brookes; the Bruce family; Clarabella Burley; Lauren Calleja; Troy Caltaux; Rachael Calvert; the Campbell family; Jon and Naomi Casimir; Mathew Cribb; the Currie-Lowe family; Gemma Dallyn; Neal Danby; Severine Demanet; Doug Dehmer; Mike Dierlinger; the Donovan family; Jill Dupleix for her sage advice at the outset; Terry Durack; Ruth Emery; Lochie Fargher; the Fassnidge family; Nigel Foster; Ian Frith; James Gardner; Greg Gibson; Nicole Gilliver; Polly Gollings; Kadla Gonthier; John Govich; Michael Gray; Kate Gresham; Christopher Hagan; Athalia and Henry Harper; Margie Harris; Nina Harris and Deborah Solomon; Stevie Hawke-Morphett; Angela Hede; the Hedley family; the Holloway family and the staff at Nu Nu; Marni Holuigue; the Hong family; the Hosking family; Graham Hudson; Dan Hunt and his fantastic fishing boat; Josephine Jagger-Manners; Suwan Jeffery; Ronni Kahn and everyone at OzHarvest; Beat Keller; Rachel Kelly; Tina Kelly; Hannah Kirkpatrick; Christine Knight; Koori Job Ready; Kathryn Larsen; the Lau family; the Leong family; Monica Leong and baby Lucy-Belle; Darren Lewis; the Lord family; the McConnell family; Caroline McCredie; Jo McGann; Kayla McGrath; Peter 'Marcho' Marchant; the good looking crew of the *Mar Tirreno C*; Natascha Mirosch; the sisterhood of The Monday Morning Cooking Club; Patrick and Vivienne Ness; Sir Ralph Norris; Angela McKue and the staff at The O'Connell Inn; Harold O'Donohue Valencia; Ruth Oliphan; the O'Meara family (especially Finnigan 'The Dude'); the Ousby family; Simone Panayiotakopoulos; the Patrick family; Michelle Pattison; Sam, Macy and Indy Perry; Garry Phipps; Winnie Chan and the great sports at the Prairie Hotel who drank beer in the cold to get the shot; the Puglisi family; Scott Pullyblank; Cathy Radke; Sam Rodely; Janet Russell-Clarke; the extended Salloum family; Tara Seymour; Shangri-La Hotel Sydney and their gangsta pastry team; Clayton Sim; Dan Sims; James Startup; Shivnesh Sumer; John Susman; Remy Tancred; Richard Taylor; Sharon Timms; Mike Tod; Pauline and Tim Tresise; John and Helen Tunbridge; Cheryl Turner; Rob Vesty; Countess Miriam von Keyserlingk-Eberius; Anthea Waller; Darren Whaites; Sharlee Gibb and the Wilkinson hooligans; the Wilson family; Larissa Wolf-Tasker; Mr Woo; Chris Wotton; Danielle Wren and Stephanie Young.

Huge thanks to Geoff Blackwell, Ruth Hobday and the staff at PQ Blackwell; and Murray Thom, Anne Thom, Wendy Nixon and Mary Wells at Thom Productions.

And finally, to everyone and their teams who said 'yes' to being in this book, thank you. We couldn't have done it without you.

Left to right: Melissa Leong (editor), Hayley Thom (videographer), Helen Greenwood (editor), Lottie Hedley (photographer) and Tim Harper (creative director).

EDITORS: Helen Greenwood and Melissa Leong

PUBLISHER: Geoff Blackwell

EDITOR IN CHIEF: Ruth Hobday

EXECUTIVE PRODUCER: Murray Thom

CREATIVE DIRECTOR: Tim Harper

DESIGN: Tim Harper, Bridget White

PHOTOGRAPHY: Lottie Hedley

VIDEOGRAPHY: Hayley Thom

FOOD EDITOR: Teresa McIntyre

ASSISTANT EDITOR: Abby Aitcheson

ADDITIONAL EDITORIAL: Mary Dobbyn, Diane Lowther

ADDITIONAL PRODUCTION: Helene Dehmer

ORIGINAL CONCEPT CREATED BY: Murray Thom and Tim Harper

The Great Australian Cookbook benefits Australian charity OzHarvest, which will receive a portion of the proceeds to support their inspired effort towards distributing food to people in need of help in the community: ozharvest.org

Find and follow us on:

#thegreataussiecookbook

thegreataustraliancookbook.com.au

ISBN: 978-0-473-32062-1

Printed in China by 1010 Printing Group Limited